High-Scoring Softball

Ralph Weekly
Karen Weekly

Human Kinetics

Library of Congress Cataloging-in-Publication Data

Weekly, Ralph.
  High-scoring softball / Ralph Weekly, Jr., Karen J. Weekly.
     p. cm.
  ISBN 978-1-4504-0139-5 (soft cover) -- ISBN 1-4504-0139-2 (soft cover)
  1. Softball--Training. 2. Softball--Coaching. I. Weekly, Karen J.
II. Title.
  GV881.4.T72W44 2012
  796.3578--dc23

                              2011050229

ISBN-10: 1-4504-0139-2 (print)
ISBN-13: 978-1-4504-0139-5 (print)

Acquisitions Editor: Justin Klug; **Developmental Editor:** Heather Healy; **Assistant Editor:** Claire Marty; **Copyeditor:** Patrick Connolly; **Permissions Manager:** Martha Gullo; **Graphic Designer:** Joe Buck; **Graphic Artists:** Joe Buck and Julie L. Denzer; **Cover Designer:** Keith Blomberg; **Photographer (cover):** University of Tennessee; **Photographer (interior):** Neil Bernstein, © Human Kinetics; **Photo Asset Manager:** Laura Fitch; **Visual Production Assistant:** Joyce Brumfield; **Photo Production Manager:** Jason Allen; **Art Manager:** Kelly Hendren; **Associate Art Manager:** Alan L. Wilborn; **Illustrations:** © Human Kinetics; **Printer:** United Graphics

We thank the University of Tennessee in Knoxville, Tennessee, for assistance in providing the location for the photo shoot for this book.

Human Kinetics books are available at special discounts for bulk purchase. Special editions or book excerpts can also be created to specification. For details, contact the Special Sales Manager at Human Kinetics.

Printed in the United States of America   10 9 8 7 6 5 4 3 2 1

The paper in this book is certified under a sustainable forestry program.

Human Kinetics
Website: www.HumanKinetics.com

United States: Human Kinetics
P.O. Box 5076
Champaign, IL 61825-5076
800-747-4457
e-mail: humank@hkusa.com

Canada: Human Kinetics
475 Devonshire Road Unit 100
Windsor, ON N8Y 2L5
800-465-7301 (in Canada only)
e-mail: info@hkcanada.com

Europe: Human Kinetics
107 Bradford Road
Stanningley
Leeds LS28 6AT, United Kingdom
+44 (0) 113 255 5665
e-mail: hk@hkeurope.com

Australia: Human Kinetics
57A Price Avenue
Lower Mitcham, South Australia 5062
08 8372 0999
e-mail: info@hkaustralia.com

New Zealand: Human Kinetics
P.O. Box 80
Torrens Park, South Australia 5062
0800 222 062
e-mail: info@hknewzealand.com

E5288

In loving memory of my parents, Chuck and Ruthann Kvale, who attended every game I played but never questioned the coach or stressed over my performance. Because of their example and unconditional love, softball is what I do and not who I am.

And to Ralph, my husband, friend, and mentor. My deepest thanks for your love and encouragement.

Karen

With profound thanks to my parents, my sons, John and Marc, their wives, Heidi and Cheryl, and my amazing grandchildren, Taylor, Jake, Matthew, Regan, and Garrett. Most important, I am thankful for all of God's blessings, the best of which is my wife Karen. She is the best coach, mentor, and life partner anyone could ever have. She inspires me to reach for the summit in every endeavor I undertake.

Ralph

Contents

Drill Finder

Drills	SOFTBALL SKILLS						
	Bunting	Slap hitting	Baserunning	Hitting for average	Hitting for power	Bat speed	Page
Front Toss With Wiffle Balls or Softies	✓	✓		✓			20
Bat With Catch Net	✓						20
Bunt Skills off a Machine	✓						21
Bunt Skills off Live Pitching	✓						21
Cones for Placement Targets	✓						22
Drag Bunt Contact	✓	✓					33
Drag Bunt Contact and Footwork		✓					34
Drag Bunt—Put It All Together		✓					34
Soft Slap Contact		✓					38
Soft Slap Contact and Footwork		✓					39
Soft Slap—Put It All Together		✓					39
Toss and Catch		✓					40
Wall Swing		✓		✓	✓		41
Hard Slap Contact		✓					44
Hard Slap Contact and Footwork		✓					45
Hard Slap—Put It All Together		✓					45
High-Chop Bounce		✓					47
Home to First With Breakdowns			✓				64
Home to Second With Cones			✓				65
Runners at Home, First, and Third			✓				66
Leadoff Drill			✓				67

Drills	SOFTBALL SKILLS						
	Bunting	Slap hitting	Baserunning	Hitting for average	Hitting for power	Bat speed	Page
Two-Machine Drill			✓				68
Small Bat and Ball-Side Toss				✓	✓		74
Quick Toss				✓	✓	✓	75
Pitch Recognition				✓	✓		75
Overhead Toss				✓	✓		76
Balance Beam				✓	✓		77
Bouncing Tennis Balls				✓	✓		78
Tee With String or Tee to Target				✓	✓		80
Front Toss or Live Pitching Into a Net				✓	✓		81
Triple Tee				✓	✓		82
Tennessee Zones				✓	✓		83
Tee Drill for Opposite Field				✓	✓		84
Front Toss From Close Range				✓	✓		85
No Pop, No Pull				✓	✓		85
Double Tee				✓	✓		86
1-2-3 Drill				✓	✓		96
Hip Rotation Drill				✓	✓		98
High Tee on Home Plate					✓		99
Machine and Cage Drill					✓		100
Full-Field Power Drill					✓		101
Pitching Machine at 33 Feet						✓	108
Hitting Tube						✓	108
Woofin Stix Drill						✓	109
Quick Toss With Weighted Balls						✓	109
Tee With Weighted Balls or 16-Inch Softballs						✓	110

(continued) ➠

Similarly, of the top 20 individual single-season batting averages, 19 occurred after 1988. In fact, a review of the record book reveals that 97 percent of the top single-season performances in virtually every offensive category (batting average, runs scored, hits, doubles, triples, home runs, slugging percentage, and runs batted in) occurred in the years after 1987.

Recommended Fences and Distances

In the early years of collegiate softball, not every team played on an enclosed field. For games played on a field without a fence, a double in the gap could potentially become a home run for a fast hitter; however, true power hitters had a more difficult time hitting home runs because the outfield could play as deep as they wanted in order to prevent the ball from going over their head. As more colleges sponsored fastpitch teams and built modern facilities for competition, enclosed fields became more common.

The NCAA recommends that all Division I softball programs have enclosed fields with fences no more than 235 feet from home plate. If the outfield fence is 4 feet high, the NCAA recommends that the fence distances be a minimum of 210 feet in left and right field and 230 feet in center field. If the outfield fence is at least 6 feet high, the NCAA recommends that fence distances be a minimum of 190 feet in left and right fields and 220 feet in center field. The prevalence of enclosed fields with fences meeting these recommended standards has made the home run a much bigger part of the game in the past 20 years.

Optic Yellow Ball

In 1993, another change occurred that was designed to add more offense to the game—the optic yellow ball with red stitches became the standard ball used in collegiate fastpitch, replacing the softer white ball. Not only was the yellow ball easier to see, but performance was enhanced because the traditional 88 double stitch was changed to 120 stitches, which allowed for greater spin and speed. The yellow ball was also made with a harder and more lively poly core rather than the kapok center of the traditional white ball. Statistics after 1992 suggest that the optic yellow ball was a big factor in the offensive explosion in collegiate fastpitch softball—even bigger than the increased pitching distance. In the offensive categories mentioned previously, 93 percent of the top single-season performances occurred after 1992.

Another statistic that suggests a greater impact from the introduction of the optic yellow ball is earned run average per game per team. In 1987, the earned run average per game per team was 1.86. In 1988, the first season pitching from 43 feet, that number only increased to 1.91. During the next five seasons, earned run average per game per team fluctuated from 1.82 (1989) to 2.04 (1991). However, a significant increase occurred from 1992 to 1993. The earned run average per game per team in 1992 (the last year of using the softer white ball) was 2.03. In 1993, that number jumped to 2.37, an increase of 14 percent. In the ensuing seasons, the number has never been lower than 2.44.

Composite Bats

After years of swinging aluminum bats, fastpitch players at the college level began using composite bats sometime in the early 2000s. Although we don't have hard statistics on the number of programs and players using composite bats (and when they began using them), the majority of collegiate Division I players have clearly been using composite bats in the latter half of the decade. Composite bats require a longer break-in period than aluminum bats (about 150 to 200 swings), but once broken in, these bats will outperform an aluminum bat in both distance and batted ball speed. Composite bats also become "hotter" over the life of the bat. We may end up looking back on the period of 2005 to 2010 as the "hot bat era" in college softball.

The upward trend in home runs per game in NCAA Division I softball from 2001 to 2010 supports the theory that composite bats have had a significant impact on offense. In 2001, the average number of home runs per game per team was 0.32. By 2005, when composite bats were generally available and in use by most Division I programs, that number had jumped to 0.52. Since then, home runs per game per team has not dropped below 0.55, and it reached a record high of 0.64 in the 2010 season. Average runs scored per game per team reached a new record of 4.19 in 2010 as well.

Earned run average has increased along with home runs per game. From 1982 to 1992, the earned run average per game per team ranged from a low of 1.35 (1984) to a high of 2.04 (1991). The first year of the optic yellow ball, 1993, saw this number jump to 2.37, a .34 increase from the 2.03 average in 1992. From 1994 to 2004, earned run averages fluctuated, but there was no single-season increase greater than .15. The years 2004 to 2005, however, marked a significant increase in earned run average per game per team when the number jumped from 2.62 in 2004 to 2.92 in 2005. Since 2005, the earned run average per game per team has not been below 3.00, and the high of 3.40 occurred in 2010. These numbers certainly suggest that composite bats are a major contributing factor to the record number of home runs hit and runs scored.

Note that batting averages have remained fairly steady over the same period of time. The last significant jump in team batting averages occurred from 1992 (.251) to 1993 (.265), the year the optic yellow ball was introduced. Since then, no statistically noteworthy trends either way have occurred in batting average, and the record of .272 was set in 1996, before the composite bat era. In fact, the average batting average per team was the same in 2009 as in 1993 (.265).

In 2011, the NCAA launched a mandatory bat-testing program. All bats were tested before each level of postseason competition and were required to comply with a 98 mph batted ball speed (exit speed). The 98 mph requirement had been in place before 2011, and manufacturers had to certify that each bat they produced met the 98 mph limit when it left the factory. However bat testing was conducted only after the completion of the Women's College World Series (WCWS) and only on bats used by the teams participating in the WCWS. Because composite bats become "hotter" over time, it was possible and even likely that a bat that left the factory performing at 98 mph would test higher than that during the life of the bat. Of the 24 bats tested after the 2010 WCWS, 17 exceeded the 98 mph standard. In 2011 when precompetition bat testing became mandatory during postseason play, only 1 bat of the 24 tested following completion of the WCWS exceeded the 98 mph standard. It will be interesting to see if the more stringent bat standards and testing protocols have an effect on the offensive numbers, especially home runs and runs scored.

Left-Handed Slap Game

The left-handed slap game evolved as a way to counteract the pitching dominance that was prevalent in softball for many years. The idea behind slapping is to shorten the swing and simply "touch and run." The batter is not trying to hit for power; rather, her goal is to put the ball in play and force the defense to make a defensive out. At least this puts more pressure on a defense than a strikeout! Slapping added a new and exciting element to softball, and it is now a common component of most offenses. Fans enjoy watching the speed and aggressiveness that slappers bring to an offense.

GENERAL TRENDS

When I played travel and college softball (late 1970s to mid-1980s), pitchers threw three pitches in addition to a fastball—the drop, the rise, and the changeup. The pitchers' goal was always to change planes or speeds with their pitches. The curve and screwball were unheard of; nobody threw a pitch that stayed on the same plane. After I began coaching in 1988, I observed that most umpires called a wide strike zone—calling strikes off the edges of the plate as long as the pitch was inside the chalk line. Over the next several years, I witnessed a huge increase in the number of pitchers who threw primarily screwballs and curveballs (pitches that move side to side but don't change planes). I have often wondered if the wide strike zone helped to create an era of average pitchers who were not able to change planes with their pitches but achieved success in part because of generous strike zones.

Over the last few years (since about 2009), a point of emphasis among Division I softball umpires has been to more accurately call balls and strikes. This has likely contributed to the increased offensive numbers. In 2009, umpires also increased their focus on enforcing the pitching rules, and many illegal pitch calls were made against pitchers who had never been called on it before. On an illegal pitch call, the pitch is called a ball on the batter, and any base runners are allowed to advance one base. These consequences are certain to assist the offensive team.

Coaches have also been placing a greater emphasis on hitting, especially hitting for power, in the last several years. Whether this emphasis occurred before or after the improvements in bat technology and the decline in pitching is difficult to determine. Was it a cause or an effect? An attempt to answer that would be nothing more than an opinion. Suffice it to say that offense seems to be the engine driving the game at the current time. In 2009, five of the top seven home-run hitting teams in Division I qualified for the Women's College World Series. So regardless of the reason, offense is certainly a large part of a winning formula.

This book discusses the elements of a high-scoring offense. It provides details on the skills involved in offense, the strategies that can be used to increase run production, and the mental tactics that help players perform up to their potential on offense. We hope you are as passionate about offensive softball as we are. Now, let's go score some runs!

CHAPTER 1

Bunting

The bunt is an important skill for players in a high-scoring offense. Everyone is in love with the home run, but being able to play small ball often proves to be the difference between winning and losing. Teams will encounter many situations in which they need to use the bunt and other components of small ball. When facing an excellent pitcher, a team may not be able to string together enough consecutive hits to score, or the team may believe that the chances of scoring via the home run are decreased. Sometimes teams have difficulty adjusting to a particular type of pitcher or pitch and must find other ways to manufacture runs. Softball seasons are long and encompass many games, and teams occasionally have hitting slumps. Playing small ball can help a team through those tough stretches and can ignite an otherwise stagnant offense.

Each player in the lineup—regardless of the player's speed or hitting prowess—should be able to execute the sacrifice bunt, the push bunt, the suicide squeeze, and the fake bunt and slap. Faster players will also want to learn how to execute a drag bunt.

SACRIFICE BUNT

The purpose of the sacrifice bunt is clearly indicated in its name—the batter is sacrificing herself or "giving herself up" in order to advance a runner to the next base. The sacrifice bunt is commonly used when a batter leading off an inning reaches first base. A well-executed sacrifice bunt will move the runner to second base, while the batter–runner is thrown out at first. The offensive team now has a runner in scoring position (second base) with only one out. As a result, the offense has two opportunities to score that runner with a base hit.

A sacrifice bunt may also be used when the batter leading off the inning reaches second base. In this case, the sacrifice will move the runner to third with only one out. The runner on third now has many more ways that she can score—on a base hit, on a fly ball (by tagging up and scoring), on an infield groundout, on a passed ball or wild pitch, on an illegal pitch, on a suicide squeeze, and so on.

The technique used in executing a sacrifice bunt is in many respects the same as for the subsequent bunts discussed in this chapter (i.e., the drag, push, and squeeze bunts). Variations in technique required to execute the other bunts are specifically noted in the descriptions of those bunts.

Technique

The batter can use one of two methods of footwork to get in a good position to bunt—the square-around method or the pivot method. With either method, the batter starts in a good hitting position with both feet even with her shoulders and with her toes pointed toward home plate (she is squared up to the plate; see figure 1.1). In the square-around method, the batter moves her right foot

Figure 1.1 Batter squared up to the plate.

Figure 1.2 Batter squared around.

toward the plate and points her toes toward the pitcher (see figure 1.2). She moves her left foot back even with her right foot and also points her toes toward the pitcher. In this position, the batter's feet are about shoulder-width apart or slightly wider, and her hips and chest are open to the pitcher. By squaring around, the batter has moved from being squared up to the plate to being squared up to the pitcher.

In the pivot method, the batter pivots on both feet so that her toes are pointed toward the pitcher (see figure 1.3). Her hips and chest should also now be open to the pitcher; the batter's left foot is in front, and her right foot is farther back in the batter's box. To make sure she can cover the outside portion of the strike zone, the batter should move closer to the inside chalk line of the batter's box.

Whether a batter chooses to use the square-around or pivot method when bunting is typically a matter of personal preference, or the coach may suggest one or the other depending on the player's success in executing the bunt play. One advantage of the square-around method is that it helps ensure that the batter gets

Figure 1.3 Batter pivoting.

her chest and hips open to the pitcher, which increases her chances of getting the bat barrel out in front. A disadvantage of the square-around method is that the batter must begin her movements early enough to get her feet in this position, thus showing the defense earlier that she is going to bunt.

An advantage of the pivot method is that the batter does not have to pick up and replace her feet; therefore, she can show the bunt later than with the square-around method. A disadvantage is that, because her feet are in a running position, the batter may have a tendency to move toward first base before she executes the bunt. Doing so will decrease her chances of getting the bunt down.

Regardless of which footwork method is used, the batter should make sure she is positioned in the front part of the batter's box when she makes contact (see figure 1.4). This will increase her opportunity to bunt the ball in fair territory. The batter should also bend her knees slightly so that she is in a relaxed, athletic position and is able to adjust to pitches in all areas of the strike zone.

As the batter moves her feet into a good bunting position, she should slide her top hand up the bat as far as possible while still being comfortable (see figure 1.5). At a minimum, she must go as high as where the handle becomes the barrel. Controlling the barrel is essential in executing a sacrifice bunt. The farther the batter's hand is placed toward the end of the barrel, the more control she will have when the ball hits the bat. If the batter's top hand is not up the barrel, the sheer speed of the pitched ball will cause the barrel to snap back and decrease the batter's chances of bunting the ball on the ground and in fair territory. The bottom hand should remain near the knob of the bat on the bat grip. Separation of the two hands allows for greater bat control.

Figure 1.4 Batter positioned in the front of the box.

Figure 1.5 Proper hand placement for the sacrifice bunt.

Young players often hesitate to place their top hand on the barrel of the bat because they are afraid of getting hit by the ball. For these players, a good technique is making a thumbs-up fist (see figure 1.6) with the top hand and gripping the barrel with it. This should keep their thumb on top and behind the barrel while their remaining fingers stay below the barrel, thus avoiding being in a position to get hit. Although some players are comfortable placing their entire hand around the barrel, coaches should not teach this to young players.

The bat should be level with the top of the strike zone (or the armpits) and almost parallel to the ground (see figure 1.7); *almost parallel* means that the barrel may be slightly higher than the knob of the bat in the ready position. Most batters have a tendency to drop the barrel a little when they make contact; therefore, if they start with the barrel slightly higher, the bat should be parallel to the ground at the time of contact. The elbows are bent at about a 90-degree angle. This keeps the bat out in front of the batter so that she can easily track the ball with her eyes, and it helps ensure that the ball is bunted fair.

The batter should be slightly bent at the waist with her head and eyes just above and looking over the top of the barrel. From this position, the batter simply wants to "catch" the ball on the barrel—she should not push out, pull in, or drop the barrel at contact. The batter should move for pitches lower in the strike zone by bending the knees, not by dropping the barrel (see figure 1.8 on page 12). With the bat positioned at the top of the strike zone, the batter should never have to go up in order to bunt a strike. This bat position also serves as a good guide, allowing the batter to know that pitches thrown

Figure 1.6 The thumbs-up fist.

Figure 1.7 Proper bat position.

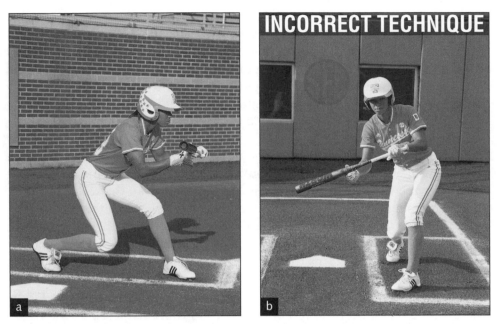

Figure 1.8 For low pitches, the correct technique is for the batter *(a)* to bend the knees rather than *(b)* dropping the barrel.

higher than the bat are not in the strike zone. Because the object of a sacrifice bunt is to advance a base runner, the batter must bunt the ball on the ground. A pop-up will not help in this situation. Batters must remember the following points in order to get the bunt down on the ground:

- **Keep the feet planted at contact.** Batters often get anxious and start moving out of the box before contact, resulting in a mis-hit or pop-up. To prevent this, coaches can tell their players to pretend that their feet are stuck in concrete. Another cue that may be used is "appreciate, then accelerate," which means that the batter should stay still and appreciate a well-executed sacrifice bunt before she starts to move toward first base. Remember, the batter is *sacrificing* herself in order to move the base runner, not trying to bunt for a base hit.

- **Keep the barrel of the bat level at contact.** Dropping the barrel is the cause of many popped-up bunt attempts. The batter must keep the barrel level and must adjust with her legs if she needs to reach a pitch low in the strike zone. Getting around early enough to get set in a good bunting position will help to prevent any late or extra movement with the barrel that could cause a pop-up.

- **Keep the barrel of the bat still at contact.** Batters may tend to straighten their arms and jab at the ball at contact, or they may pull the arms in and give with the ball at contact. Both of these movements increase the chances of a mis-hit or pop-up. To emphasize the importance of keeping the barrel still, coaches can tell batters to pretend that there is a glove on the end of the bat and to try to "catch" the ball with that glove. Batters often mistakenly think that giving with the ball will deaden the ball coming off the bat. This is not the proper technique to use when the batter wants to deaden the ball. The key to having the ball come off the bat soft is to bunt the ball on the last 5 inches (12.7 cm) of the barrel, thus avoiding the bat's sweet spot where the ball tends to come off harder.

- **Maintain good barrel control.** Too many batters attempt to bunt with both hands on the bottom part of the bat or with the hands placed too closely together. When using these hand positions, batters have no control over the barrel. The speed of a pitch (often 55 miles per hour or more) will cause the batter's barrel to snap back and drop if she doesn't position her hands properly. For the batter to maintain sufficient control, the top hand must be somewhere on the barrel of the bat, and the hands must be separated (see figure 1.9).

Once players have mastered the basic technique for the sacrifice bunt, they can begin to work on hiding the bunt from the defense for as long as possible. There is a fine line here. If the player tries to hide the bunt too long, she may end up squaring around too late and not getting the bat and her body in position to execute the sacrifice bunt. The key to creating deception is to wait as long as possible to make the initial move to bunt, and then to move the feet and barrel into bunt position as quickly as possible. Considerable practice is required for players to master the timing that enables them to be deceptive and still deliver a successful sacrifice bunt.

Figure 1.9 (a) Proper hand position for good barrel control. (b) Incorrect hand position that provides no control over the barrel.

Placement

To have a chance of moving the base runner into scoring position, the batter must bunt the ball into fair territory. A few key strategies will help the batter keep the bunt fair. As mentioned previously, one key is for the batter to position herself in the front of the batter's box. Another key is to make sure the elbows are bent equally and at approximately 90 degrees (see figure 1.10*a*). Straightening one arm while keeping the other bent (figure 1.10*b*) will create a barrel angle pointing sharply toward either the first- or third-base line. A final strategy is to bunt pitches that are strikes. It is much easier to bunt a pitch in the strike zone into fair territory than a pitch outside of the zone. Additionally, a batter shouldn't sacrifice an out if she can advance the base runner on first and get to first base herself on a walk.

Besides making sure that the bunt is fair, the batter needs to focus on the specific placement of the bunt in order to successfully advance the base runner. A bunter should develop the ability to place the ball in an area that will exploit a weakness or avoid a strength in the infield defense. For example, with a runner on first, the batter should not bunt directly to the third-base player if that player is a strong defensive player and is playing close to the plate in an attempt to force the base runner at second. Always remember that the primary goal is to move the base runner. Generally, a good strategy is to bunt the ball to the area in front of home plate that is equally distant from the pitcher, the catcher, and the first- and third-base players (see figure 1.11).

Figure 1.10 *(a)* Correct arm position for good placement of the bunt. *(b)* Poor arm position results in poor placement.

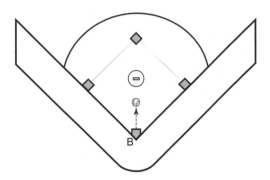

Figure 1.11   The best location for placing bunts.

This creates a situation where four defensive players are forced to communicate regarding who is going to make the play, which increases the potential for miscommunication.

DRAG BUNT FROM THE RIGHT SIDE

Drag bunting from the right side is a skill that is rarely used in softball, yet it can be very effective. Unlike the sacrifice bunt, the goal of a drag bunt is to get a hit and to get on base. The element of surprise is the key factor in executing a drag bunt. Therefore, the batter needs to show the drag bunt as late as possible in order to keep the defense off balance. In addition, the batter must have better-than-average speed to successfully execute a drag bunt.

Technique

Because deception and surprise are critical to the success of a drag bunt, the batter must move quickly to get the barrel in position to bunt. The batter should not move her feet before doing this. She brings the knob of the bat toward her left hip while at the same time sliding her right hand up the bat to where the barrel begins (see figure 1.12 on page 16). Separating her hands like this will ensure good barrel control at contact (similar to when executing a sacrifice bunt). As contact is made, the batter steps with her right foot to initiate the race to first base (see figure 1.13 on page 16).

Placement and Strategy

The goal of the drag bunt is getting on base, so the batter should place the ball in an area that gives her the greatest chance of being safe. This may be toward the defensive player (first- or third-base player) who is playing farthest from home plate, or it may be toward the player who is the slowest in reacting to the ball. If the batter has identified the weakest defensive player between the corner fielders and the pitcher, she may elect to challenge that player's skills. The skill level of the pitcher, as well as the location of the pitch, may

Figure 1.12 Proper hand position for the drag bunt.

Figure 1.13 Stepping to initiate the run to first base.

prevent the batter from having a great degree of control over where the bunt eventually lands. Again, deception and the player's speed are key elements.

Batters should use the drag bunt when the defense least expects it. Coaches and defensive players often anticipate a drag bunt when a right-handed batter with above-average speed comes to the plate, especially when that batter is hitting near the top or bottom of the order. The batter may show "swing away" on the first pitch or two in order to convince the defense that she is hitting away, thus forcing the corners to move away from the plate. A great time to execute a drag bunt (or any other skill that relies on the element of surprise) is right after a defensive mistake. Look for situations where the defense is anxious or frustrated about what just happened on the field or in the flow of the game. These are the times when a batter may be able to catch the defense off guard.

PUSH BUNT

The push bunt is a great tool to use when a batter needs to move a runner and the defense is expecting a sacrifice bunt. The batter does everything just as she would when executing a sacrifice bunt. However, at the point of contact, the batter pushes the ball so that it travels faster and farther than a sacrifice bunt.

Technique

For the push bunt, the push should be generated by the lower body. In her pivot bunt position, the batter shifts her weight to her right leg. As the ball is about to strike the bat, the batter shifts her weight forward to her left leg, thereby generating the push and momentum to bunt the ball harder. The barrel moves as the batter's weight shifts. A common mistake that batters make when attempting a push bunt is to push the barrel out with their arms and not their legs. This causes too much movement with the barrel, which increases the chances of a miss or mis-hit. For a push bunt the batter should make contact on the barrel's sweet spot in order to bunt the ball harder.

Placement and Strategy

A push bunt is best used when the defense is overreacting to a sacrifice bunt and getting out of position. A defense is most vulnerable to the push bunt when they are aggressively defending the sacrifice bunt in an attempt to force the out at second base. For example, if the corner players are charging hard when they see the batter take up a bunt position, the batter may push the bunt past them. If the second-base player breaks to cover first base too early, she may leave a hole on the right side of the infield and provide a perfect spot for a push bunt (see figure 1.14). This may also happen with the shortstop, who may break too quickly to cover second base and leave a similarly large hole on the left side of the infield (figure 1.14). On a well-executed push bunt, the ball should travel too fast for a corner player to move laterally to field the ball, but it should travel too slowly for a middle infielder to adjust and field the ball in time to make an out.

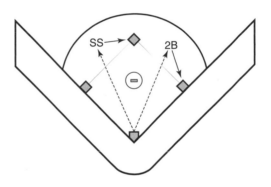

Figure 1.14 Key placements for the push bunt when infielders move out of position early.

FAKE BUNT AND SLAP

Like the push bunt, the fake bunt and slap is most effective when the defense is aggressively attempting to defend the sacrifice bunt. The batter shows bunt, and as the defense charges toward home plate to defend the bunt, the batter pulls back and slaps the ball past the corner players or to an area vacated by a defensive player moving to cover a base.

Technique

When executing a fake bunt and slap, the batter takes up a sacrifice bunt position. She must do this early enough so that she can "sell" bunt to the defense.

Remember, in the sacrifice bunt position, the batter's hips and chest are open to the pitcher. As the pitcher releases the ball, the batter slides her hands together at the top of the grip and brings the barrel back far enough to take a short swing at the ball (see figure 1.15). The batter should not bring the barrel back into a full hitting position. Doing so would require too much time and would negate the element of surprise. A good guide for the slap position is to make sure that the batter's chest and hips are facing the second-base player; the batter shouldn't close any farther than that.

By sliding her hands up to the top of the grip, the batter has a shorter bat to work with and therefore has greater bat control. This should allow her to better place the ball when she performs the slap. The slap swing is short and level, and it must have a follow-through. A common mistake that players make when attempting the fake bunt and slap is to stop the barrel at contact. This often results in a pop-up or foul ball. Batters should maintain a short, level swing and should follow through by rolling their top hand. This should keep the ball on the ground. Another common mistake is to chop down at the ball rather than swing level. Chopping down decreases the opportunity to make solid contact with the ball. A level swing increases the likelihood of making contact and hitting the ball on the ground. A good visual cue for the batter is to aim for the top half of the ball while swinging level.

Figure 1.15   Proper hand and barrel position for the fake bunt and slap.

Placement and Strategy

The fake bunt and slap is a great tool when the defense is overplaying the bunt. If the first- and third-base players are charging aggressively to defend the anticipated bunt, the batter may catch them off balance by pulling the bat back to slap the ball past them. In this situation, the batter will want to slap the ball hard right at the charging corner player (see figure 1.16a).

The fake bunt and slap is also an excellent weapon when the middle infielders (shortstop and second-base player) are anticipating a bunt and vacating their positions early to cover the bases (see figure 1.16b). In this case, the best placement for the slap is to the area normally occupied by the shortstop or second-base player in her defensive positioning.

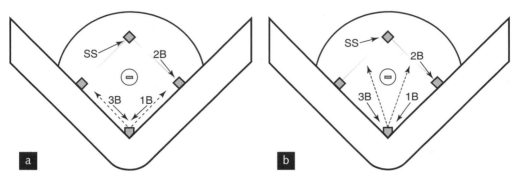

Figure 1.16 Good placement choices for the slap when *(a)* the first- and third-base players and *(b)* the middle infielders fall for the fake bunt.

SQUEEZE BUNT (SUICIDE SQUEEZE)

One of our favorite plays is the squeeze bunt, or suicide squeeze. This play is a good option when the team has a fast runner on third base and a good bunter at the plate. Some of our best bunters have also been power hitters, and the defense is usually caught off guard when a power hitter executes a squeeze bunt. Running a squeeze play certainly involves an element of risk, because the runner on third is heading home on the pitch; the batter must get the bunt down or foul it off in order to avoid forcing the runner at third into an easy out. A coach has to be willing to take that risk, and knowing the team and their ability to execute the play will minimize the risk.

Technique

The suicide squeeze technique is the same as that for a sacrifice bunt. The only difference is that the batter may need to wait a little longer to show bunt in order to deceive the infield defense. However, the batter must not wait so long that she is unable to get the barrel on the ball and get the bunt down. Timing is critical on this play. Batters will need a lot of practice to get the timing perfected to where they have confidence in their ability to successfully execute the squeeze bunt.

Remember, the batter does not have the option of bunting or not bunting the ball as she does in a sacrifice situation. She must attempt to bunt the ball no matter where the pitch is located. Even if the pitch is over her head or rolling on the ground, she must at least foul it off. The runner is leaving third without hesitation when the pitch is released and will run into a catcher's tag if the batter doesn't make contact with the ball.

Placement and Strategy

A suicide squeeze is a great play when a team is facing a good pitcher and is having difficulty scoring via a base hit. Early in the game, the team may want to use this play to seize the offensive momentum and to get on the scoreboard; in this situation, the team is often willing to give up playing for the possible big inning. A successful squeeze play guarantees scoring one run. And who knows, this play may lead to a big inning anyway if the defense gets frustrated by it and loses focus for the rest of the inning.

BUNTING DRILLS

Bunting is an art that all players can and should master, regardless of their individual attributes or skill level. The ability to execute a bunt may be the difference between a win and a loss. The following drills will help hitters become more proficient with the various types of bunts.

FRONT TOSS WITH WIFFLE BALLS OR SOFTIES

Purpose   The purpose of this drill is to allow beginning bunters to become comfortable with the proper technique. Young players often worry about being hit by the ball when they are bunting. Using Wiffle balls or softie balls minimizes the players' fear and allows them to learn proper bunting mechanics.

Execution   A coach or partner tosses balls to the batter. The batter executes bunts using the proper technique for the type of bunt she is working on. Initially, the batter may start with her body and bat already in a contact position for the bunt; this will enable her to work on seeing the ball off the bat and to learn proper balance, arm position, and barrel angle. When she is comfortable making contact, the batter may advance to beginning the drill from a normal batting stance position and moving into the contact position. The batter should complete two sets of 10 repetitions or until the coach evaluates the batter as proficient.

Coaching Points   Make sure the batter is keeping her feet still on a sacrifice bunt and is maintaining a good barrel angle at contact.

BAT WITH CATCH NET

Purpose   This drill helps the batter learn the technique of letting the ball hit the bat as if she were catching the ball on the end of the bat (rather than pushing or jabbing at the ball as contact is made).

Execution   A coach or partner pitches balls to the batter. The pitches may be delivered via soft toss or a machine. (This drill should not be done using a live pitcher throwing at gamelike speed.) The batter uses a special bat that is made with a catch net on the end of the barrel. The batter catches the pitches in the net. The batter should complete two sets of 10 repetitions.

Coaching Points   If the batter maintains a good barrel angle, she will catch the ball in the net. If not, she will likely miss the ball or hit it off of some portion of the bat other than the net. Remind the batter to bend her legs for low strikes.

BUNT SKILLS OFF A MACHINE

Purpose   Once a batter has established good fundamentals by practicing bunting off front toss, she can progress to bunting off a machine with the ball coming at her faster.

Execution   Using the proper technique for the type of bunt being practiced, the batter bunts balls thrown from a pitching machine. The machine allows the batter to work on bunting pitches that are thrown at speeds similar to what she will see in a game. The batter should complete two sets of 10 repetitions.

Coaching Points   The batter may start in the contact position for the bunt until she is comfortable with the speed of the pitch; she can then progress to starting in a normal batting stance and moving into the contact position. If the player's mechanics begin to break down because of the increased speed, she should return to front-toss drills until she is more comfortable and consistent with proper bunting fundamentals.

BUNT SKILLS OFF LIVE PITCHING

Purpose   This drill allows the player to execute bunts under conditions that closely resemble what she will face in an actual game.

Execution   A pitcher throws pitches to the batter at the same speed and with the same movement that the batter will see in an actual game. Using the proper mechanics (as learned in earlier drills), the batter must execute the bunts at game speed. The batter should complete two sets of 10 repetitions or continue until the coach ends the drill.

Coaching Points   Again, the batter may start in a bunt contact position at the beginning of the drill and then progress to moving into that position from a normal batting stance. The key is to make sure that the batter has learned proper mechanics—and that those mechanics have become habits—before the batter attempts to execute them versus a live pitcher.

CONES FOR PLACEMENT TARGETS

Purpose　In this drill, batters attempt to bunt balls to desired areas on the field. The drill helps batters learn to adjust the barrel angle of the bat in order to change the placement of the bunt. This is a great drill for working on directing and deadening the ball to make it land in certain areas.

Execution　Set up cones to create a target area where the batters will try to get their bunts to land (see figure 1.17). For example, a coach may want the batters to bunt balls directly toward the pitcher in an area that is an equal distance from the pitcher, catcher, and corner players. In this case, the cones would be set up to create a visual target in that area. The target area can be changed so that batters work on bunting to various areas. A pitcher throws pitches to the batter at game speed. The batter uses proper mechanics to bunt the ball to the designated area. The batter should complete two sets of 10 or continue the drill until the coach is satisfied with the results.

Coaching Points　Players can compete with one another to see how many targets they can successfully reach with their bunts.

Figure 1.17　Drill action.

CHAPTER 2

Slap Hitting

Shortly after we became co-head coaches at the University of Tennessee, we realized the importance of including slapping in our offense. To compete at the highest level of Division I softball, we needed to be able to put the ball in play and create run-scoring opportunities against the best pitchers in the country. The three-run home run doesn't always happen against the top pitchers. Power hitters tend to slump on occasion, but speed never goes in a slump.

An offense must have the ability to play small ball and to score with slap hitting, bunting, and base stealing. Slap hitting is an exciting and necessary element of a high-scoring offense. This chapter discusses short-game techniques—including the drag bunt, the soft slap, the hard slap, and the high-chopper slap (also known as the chop slap)—and the proper fundamentals for executing these techniques. The chapter provides drills to help players improve these skills, tips on how and when to use each skill, and short-game strategies to help a team score runs.

For a team to be successful in the short game, slapping and drag bunting must be a part of the offensive philosophy. Our team always has two or three slappers in the lineup, and on occasion, we have included four slappers because this gave us the best opportunity to score runs. The slappers become a team within a team and take great pride in the strengths they bring to the offense—getting on base and creating pressure on the defense with their speed. Our slappers always work together and share ideas and tips on how to become better with their short-game skills. They support one another in their efforts. Yet, they also compete with each other on a daily basis, and there is nothing like competition to make players sharpen their skills.

The goal of the short game is to put pressure on the defense by forcing them to move in all directions and to make defensive plays quickly. A slapper must have good speed. At the highest levels of softball, many slappers can run from home to first in under 2.7 seconds (timing from contact with the bat to contact with the base). Against that kind of speed, the defense must be able to field and throw very quickly in order to make outs. A defense that is under pressure to execute fast tends to rush plays and make errors. Thus, slappers should never be concerned about batting average. The key statistic for a slapper is on-base percentage. The slapper's job is to get on base any way she can, whether by a walk, error, or base hit. Generally, the slapper's goal is to put the ball on the ground and force the defense to field *and* throw. Strikeouts and pop-ups don't put pressure on the defense, nor do they create many opportunities for errors.

Once on base, the slapper can use her speed to steal bases and continue to create problems for the defense. The simple threat of a stolen base can cause defensive players to vacate their position early and open holes for the batter. The numerous options presented by speed players cause defensive players to think too much on the field. When athletes are thinking rather than reacting, they tend to make mistakes.

FOOTWORK

The short game is designed to create a footrace to first base between the speedy slapper and the first-base player, who is typically much slower. The slapper starts moving her feet in the batter's box before she hits the ball. The slapper's goal is to be moving at contact and to maintain that momentum through contact so that she can get to first base as quickly as possible. Regardless of the short-game skill involved, the footwork for the slapper remains consistent.

The slapper starts with her toes pointed toward home plate in the left-side batter's box. She may then do one of two things with her right foot to initiate her footwork (see figure 2.1). One option is to pivot on her right foot and turn this foot so that her toe is pointing slightly left (shortstop side) of the pitcher. The other option is to slide her right foot back in the box—closer to her left foot—*and* pivot and turn the right foot so that her toe is pointing slightly left of the pitcher. Either option is acceptable.

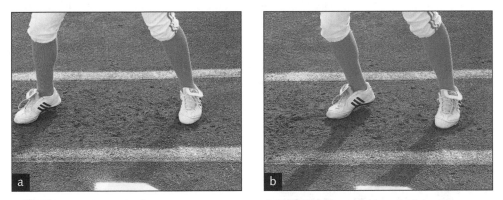

Figure 2.1   The right foot may *(a)* pivot or *(b)* slide back and pivot before the crossover step.

After this move with her right foot, the slapper brings her left foot across to the front of the batter's box, making sure that her toes are pointed toward the area slightly left of the pitcher (see figure 2.2). This is called the *crossover step*. On the crossover, the slapper wants to be sure that her left foot lands in the front inside corner of the batter's box. This is important because the slapper wants to reach first base as quickly as possible, and getting to the front of the batter's box will cut down the distance she must run to first base after making contact with the ball.

Figure 2.2   The crossover step.

Where the slapper starts in the batter's box depends on whether she pivots on her right foot only or whether she slides back and pivots. She must find the place in the box that allows her to get to the front inside line on her crossover step with whichever pivot method she uses. Her setup, pivot or pivot and slide, and crossover step must be consistent every time. Regardless of the pivot method used, the slapper should never start in the back of the batter's box; her positioning should always be somewhere between even with the plate and slightly in front of the plate (figure 2.3).

Figure 2.3 Proper starting position so that the slapper ends up in the proper place after the crossover step.

On the crossover step, the slapper needs to maintain two parallel lines with her feet (see figure 2.4*a*). A common mistake that slappers make is to cross over with the left foot directly in front of the right foot, almost as if they are running on a balance beam (see figure 2.4*b*). This creates obvious balance problems. The crossover step can be compared to the first step of jogging or running—people run with their feet on two parallel lines, and slappers should cross over in the same manner. A good beginning drill is to have the slappers stand in the batter's box

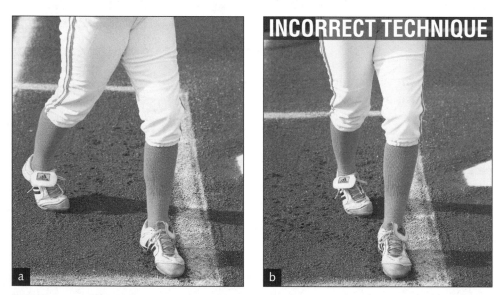

Figure 2.4 The slapper's feet should be on (*a*) parallel lines not (*b*) as if they were on a balance beam.

facing home plate, with or without a bat in their hands. Place a cone 8 to 10 feet (2.4 to 3.0 m) to the left of the pitcher (see figure 2.5). Tell the slapper to jog to the cone. The slapper will naturally pivot and cross over on two parallel lines, just as described.

When players jog or run, they should maintain a position in which their nose is over the toes of the front foot. For most people, this occurs naturally, but slappers may need to be reminded to keep their nose over their toes (see figure 2.6*a* on page 28). A common mistake made by slappers is to stand up too straight on the crossover and thus lose good running posture (see figure 2.6*b* on page 28). Remember, the advantage to slapping is that the batter is running when contact is made so that she can get a head start to first base. The slapper who stands up too tall—thus having poor running posture and form—will be slower through the box and will therefore negate her speed advantage. Keeping the nose over the toes is especially important when drag bunting and soft slapping. For reasons that will be apparent later in the chapter (see the Hard Slap section on page 41), a batter using the hard slap will usually not maintain the nose-over-toes posture all the way through the hard slap.

When some slappers take the crossover step, instead of turning their toes toward the shortstop, they point them toward home plate (see figure 2.6*c* on page 28). We refer to these players as carioca slappers because this foot position causes them to use footwork that looks as if they are performing the carioca conditioning drill. There is no benefit to slapping with the feet in this position. The whole idea of slapping is to run to first base as quickly as possible after contact. If a batter's feet are pointed toward home, she will have a difficult time getting to first base quickly. Instead, the slapper should point her toes and jog in the direction the ball is coming from (the pitcher). Then she only has to make a slight turn with her feet toward first base after contact, rather than a complete 180-degree turn.

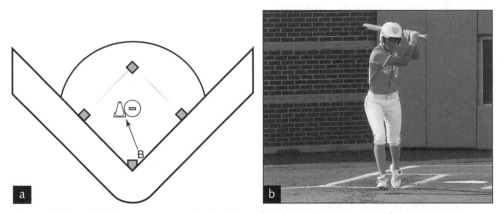

Figure 2.5 *(a)* The cone setup for helping slappers *(b)* to practice the correct footwork.

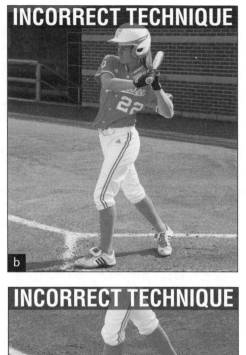

Figure 2.6   Slappers need *(a)* a proper nose over toes position rather than *(b)* standing up too straight or *(c)* using a carioca step.

TIMING FOR CONTACT AND FEET

The timing of the contact with the ball determines when a slapper needs to start her feet. Contact should occur almost simultaneously with the left foot landing on the crossover step. In reality, contact usually occurs immediately after the left foot lands, which is fine. If the slapper attempts to time her footwork so that she is making contact when the left foot lands, she will be able to maintain good momentum at the time of contact and immediately run to first base. The error that slappers tend to make is having the left foot land too early and before contact. When slappers make this error, one of two things usually occurs: The slapper instinctively pauses to wait for the ball, or she keeps her feet moving but is leaning toward first base by the time contact is made, also called pulling out. Whenever a slapper is pulling out, the first thing to look at is the timing between the contact with the ball and the landing of the crossover step.

Slappers need to start their feet so that the left foot lands at the time contact is made with the ball. Perfecting this timing takes a lot of practice. And a slapper must always remember that it is better to be late than early. Being early causes the slapper to stop or pull out, both of which are bad technique. Slappers are often trying to hit the ball in the hole between the third-base player and the shortstop, and that is very difficult to do if the slapper is early and the barrel gets out in front of the plate too soon. A general guideline is that the slapper should start just before the pitcher releases the ball. This will depend on whether the slapper uses a straight pivot and crossover or whether she likes to slide her right foot back as she pivots. The more time the crossover takes, the earlier the slapper will have to start, and vice versa. Therefore, the best strategy is to focus on good timing between crossover landing and contact, and then work backward from there to find the right starting point.

HAND POSITION

When a slapper takes her batting stance in the box, the position of her hands is no different from that of a regular batter swinging away. As shown in figure 2.7, her hands are even with or above her back shoulder; her elbows are relaxed, and she has a comfortable grip on the bat, holding the bat loosely at the base of her fingers (not buried in her palms). People frequently ask me if or how far a slapper should choke up on the bat. My answer is always the same: A slapper should choke up as far as she needs to in order to maintain good control of the barrel.

Figure 2.7 A variety of grips, *(a)* choking up, *(b)* hands at the bottom, or *(c)* hands starting at the bottom and moving up at the crossover step, work for slap hitting.

Because the slapper's goal is usually to put the ball on the ground, she must be able to keep the barrel above the ball in order to avoid pop-ups. Slappers occasionally worry that choking up on the bat (figure 2.7a) will let the defense know that they are slapping. The defense likely already knows that the player is a slapper, but they don't know whether the slapper is going to drag bunt, soft slap, or hard slap. Choking up doesn't give anything away, and the slapper should not be afraid to choke up if "shortening the bat" helps her maintain barrel control.

I have worked with many slappers, and they all did something a little different. Some choked up when they first started slapping and gradually moved their hands down the bat (figure 2.7b) as they became stronger and more experienced at maintaining barrel control. Others choked up on the bat for their entire careers. Others held the bat at the bottom of the grip and moved their hands up as they crossed over in order to maintain barrel control for a particular skill (e.g., bunt or soft slap; figure 2.7c). Coaches should work with each player individually to help her find a position that is natural and comfortable.

LEARNING PROGRESSION

The order in which a player learns short-game techniques is very important in developing a slapper's ability to execute all of the skills. Much like building a house, the foundation must be solid before the builder can even think about the walls and the roof. Too many players get impatient and want to learn everything at once or want to execute an entire skill before they have adequately learned the pieces separately. For a beginning slapper or a slapper who is learning a new skill set, the best plan is to patiently follow the progression outlined in this section.

Beginning slappers should learn the skills involved in the short game in the following sequence: drag bunt, soft slap, hard slap. The drag bunt is the foundation of the short game, and the other skills build off the drag bunt. In addition, the drag bunt should be the easiest skill to execute because the bat is stationary at contact. Barrel control becomes more challenging with the soft slap and the hard slap. Slappers who learn the hard slap first tend to pull out because they get in the bad habit of swinging too hard. The learning curve will be faster if the slapper can first learn the basic skills of drag bunting and then add to them by learning the soft slap and then the hard slap.

The slapper should use a sequenced progression of drills when learning each skill. The drill progressions in the upcoming skill sections begin with a stationary drill that enables the slapper to learn proper balance and hand mechanics. The drills then progress to having the slapper move through the batter's box while executing the skill. Last, the drills require the slapper to run the play out through first base. Slappers should not advance to the next drill in the progression until they are able to consistently execute the one before it with proper mechanics.

DRAG BUNT

The drag bunt is an essential tool for a complete slapper. The threat of the drag bunt forces the infield corner players to move closer to the plate, thereby opening up more infield gaps to slap through. The footwork described earlier for the crossover step should be used for the drag bunt.

Technique

During the crossover step, the slapper should slide her top (left) hand up the bat as far as possible while remaining comfortable (see figure 2.8a). The bottom (right) hand should remain near the knob of the bat on the grip. Separating the two hands allows for greater bat control. The slapper wants to bring her bottom hand to her right side and keep it close to her body. A common mistake made in bunting is to extend the bottom hand away from the body too much (see figure 2.8b). This causes the barrel to angle toward foul territory, and the batter will bunt the ball foul.

Slappers should have the barrel at the top of the strike zone when they bring it into the contact area. This gives them a guideline for identifying the strike zone. If the barrel is at the top of the zone, the slapper knows that any pitch above the barrel is a ball and that she should let it go. If a pitch is below the barrel but above the knees, the pitch is a strike, and the slapper may want to bunt it. For a low pitch, the slapper will bend her knees to bring the barrel down to the height of the pitch. She does not want to drop the bat head because that will increase her chances of popping up the ball.

Figure 2.8 *(a)* Proper hand position and barrel angle and *(b)* poor technique.

At contact, the bat should be level in the zone; the barrel should be even with the handle or slightly out in front. Keeping the barrel out in front of the handle will help ensure that the ball is bunted fair. The slapper needs to "catch" the ball on the bat and should not try to push, drop, or pull back the barrel of the bat. A common mistake that batters make on a drag bunt is to move the barrel at contact in an attempt to direct the ball or deaden it so that it doesn't go too far. Movement creates the opportunity for a foul ball or pop-up. To help avoid this, batters can pretend that there is a fielder's glove on the end of the bat and simply catch the ball.

Slappers can do two things to help deaden a drag bunt: slide their top hand farther up the barrel (see figure 2.9a), and bunt the ball on the top 5 inches of the bat (away from the sweet spot). An easy way to practice bunting the ball on the top 5 inches (12.7 cm) is to place a piece of tape around the barrel 5 inches from the top (figure 2.9b). The slapper must make contact in the area between the end of the bat and the tape. Another trick that some players use to help deaden bunts is to point their index finger up the barrel of the bat. (figure 2.9c).

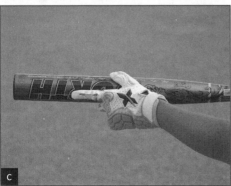

Figure 2.9 *(a)* The top hand sliding up the barrel, *(b)* tape marking the top 5 inches of the bat, and *(c)* the index finger pointing up the barrel.

Placement and Strategy

Unless the slapper is trying to bunt to a specific infielder, the ideal placement for a drag bunt is approximately 6 to 10 feet (1.8 to 3.0 m) directly in front of home plate. A drag bunt placed an equal distance from the catcher, pitcher, and third- and first-base players will require communication between all four players about who is going to field the bunt. Whenever a batter can create communication issues for the defense, she has also created the potential for miscommunication and mistakes.

The Cones for Placement Targets drill on page 22 is a great way to work on placement for the drag bunt too. Create a circle with either cones or field chalk around the area where you want the ball to be bunted; the slappers then work on placing drag bunts in that area. We like to have contests to see who can place the most bunts in the target zone. There is nothing like competition between players to increase the intensity level and performance.

Drill Progression

When learning the drag bunt, slappers should start with the most basic component, which is contacting the ball with the hands and feet in proper position. They should then progress to working on the crossover step and mastering the proper timing for that part of the skill. Finally, they should put it all together and continue to run to first base after contact. The slapper should not progress to the next drill until she has shown an ability to consistently execute the previous one in the progression.

DRAG BUNT CONTACT

Purpose   The beginning slapper must first become comfortable making contact from the left side (many slappers are right-handed batters who are converting). This includes seeing the ball from the left side, understanding the proper balance after the crossover step, practicing holding the bat correctly, and learning where to make contact on the bat.

Execution   A coach or partner uses front toss or a machine to pitch balls to the slapper. Do not use live pitching. The slapper executes the crossover step and stops in that position. Then she brings the bat to a good bunting position and performs the bunts while standing in a stationary crossed-over position. She stays in that position for the duration of the drill and makes sure that her balance is correct throughout the drill. The slapper completes two sets of 10 repetitions with a break between sets.

Coaching Points   Slappers should maintain the nose-over-toes position where the entire left foot is in contact with the ground and the right heel is in the air (like a natural running position). Also make sure that the slapper's

(continued)

Drag Bunt Contact *(continued)*

feet are on two parallel lines and not on a single line (as if on a balance beam). Slappers should not perform a stationary drill for more than 10 repetitions without a break; otherwise, they will get tired and start to "sit" with both feet flat on the ground and with the upper body upright rather than leaning slightly forward. Remember, practice does not make perfect; *perfect practice makes perfect.*

DRAG BUNT CONTACT AND FOOTWORK

Purpose This drill helps the slapper learn proper timing for the drag bunt, including when to start her crossover step so that she makes contact with the ball at the same time that her left foot lands.

Execution A coach or partner uses front toss or a machine to pitch balls to the slapper. Do not use live pitching. The slapper starts with the bat already out in front in bunting position; she crosses over when the ball is tossed so that she makes contact when her left foot lands. After contact, the slapper jogs a few steps toward the pitcher. The slapper completes two sets of 10 repetitions. When she is comfortable with the crossover step and the timing, she will start the drill with her hands in a normal batting stance position and will work on moving the barrel into bunt position as she is executing the crossover step.

Coaching Points Unless the slapper is doing stationary drills, she should keep her feet moving after contact for at least three or four steps. If the slapper stops at contact during drills, she reinforces the habit of stopping her momentum, which is one of the worst things that a slapper can do. Slappers may have to spend more time at this stage because so many important elements are being added—performing proper footwork when the ball is moving, mastering the timing at contact, continuing momentum, and learning to quickly bring the bat into drag position while crossing over. Coaches should be patient and demand proper technique before allowing a slapper to move on.

DRAG BUNT—PUT IT ALL TOGETHER

Purpose This drill lets the slapper practice the whole drag bunt sequence and run it out to first base. Players should not practice this drill until they can execute the fundamentals for the two previous drills.

Execution Several slappers line up at home plate. The coach or pitcher pitches to the first slapper using front toss. The slapper begins from a regular batting stance position and executes the drag bunt from that position, running it out through first base. The next slapper in line steps up to the plate and the first slapper jogs back to the end of the line. When slappers are comfortable performing this skill against front toss, the drill can be modified so that the pitches come from a machine and then eventually from a live pitcher.

Coaching Points   When a slapper first performs this drill, the coach should watch to make sure that she is not running toward first, or pulling out, before she makes contact with the ball. Initially, a machine or front toss should be used for this drill so that the slapper can focus on maintaining perfect fundamentals without worrying about moving pitches, locations, and changes of speed. Let the slapper get comfortable and confident with her ability to execute the drag bunt from the batter's box through first base before bringing live pitching into the drill.

Stationary Drills

Although stationary drills can be performed on a field, the majority of this drill work will likely be done in a batting cage. Here are some key pointers for doing stationary drills in a batting cage:

- The slapper needs to maintain good jogging or running posture (nose over toes) on every repetition. When slappers get tired, they often "sit" in a position where the upper body is too tall.
- After every 10 repetitions, the slapper should take a break or switch to a drill that involves moving at contact. This prevents the slapper from working in a stationary mode too long. Remember, the slap game is largely based on movement at contact.
- Each repetition should have a purpose, and visual targets can be used to help achieve this purpose. For example, the slapper can find a spot on the catch net that represents where the shortstop would play; the slapper then slaps balls to that spot.

SOFT SLAP

After the slapper learns the drag bunt, she is ready to move on to the soft slap. The soft slap is a tool that slappers can use when they want to hit the ball harder than a bunt. With this tool, the slapper also has a lot of control over the direction and speed of the ball off the bat. The swing for the soft slap is very similar to the swing used when playing a game of pepper. The swing is short, and the barrel stops at contact, giving the player the greatest opportunity to control the direction and speed of the ball. The more bounces the slapper can create before the ball reaches a fielder, the better her chance of reaching first base safely.

Technique

The footwork is the same as described previously. The hands start in a natural batting position. As mentioned earlier, whether the slapper chokes up on the bat, slides her hands up as she is moving, or keeps her hands at the bottom of the bat is a matter of personal preference. The key is that she maintains good barrel control. As the slapper crosses over, she must keep her hands up above the top of the strike zone (see figure 2.10). A lot of slappers like to keep their hands even higher by keeping them above their back shoulder; this technique also works well.

When the slapper's left foot lands after the crossover step, her weight *must* be on the ball of her left foot. This will help keep her head, shoulders, hands, and upper body in the best position possible to see the ball and cover the entire strike zone. To make contact, the slapper brings the barrel to the ball in a short, compact motion, and she stops the barrel at contact. The barrel must stay above her hands when bringing it to the contact point. Her hands stay inside the ball, moving in a direction toward the pitcher (rather than away from her body toward home plate). At the time of contact, the slapper should feel or see the following (see figure 2.11):

- The barrel is even with or above the hands.
- The hands are in front of the body and the left foot.
- The barrel is even with the left foot in order to create the angle necessary to hit the ball to short or third.

Figure 2.10 The slapper keeps her hands above the strike zone on the crossover step.

Figure 2.11 Proper positioning at contact.

A common mistake that slappers make is to swing in a severe downward arc to the ball, thinking that a downward swing will help to keep the ball on the ground. This type of swing minimizes the slapper's chances of hitting the ball, and it can even result in pop-ups when the slapper strikes the side of the ball rather than the top. Instead, slappers need to think *level* and aim for the top half of the ball. Hitting the top half of the ball will help produce the ground balls that the slapper is looking for. Keeping the hands up at the start of the swing and thinking *level* usually result in a swing with only a *slight* downward arc, which is ideal for hitting the ball on the ground.

Placement and Strategy

The slapper usually wants the soft slap to go to the shortstop or in the area between short and third (the 5-6 hole) because this creates the longest infield throw to first base (see figure 2.12). The soft slap is a great tool to use when the shortstop is playing deep. Typically, the slapper wants to avoid the right side of the infield (first- and second-base players) because those players have a short throw to first base. If any of the infielders, including the pitcher, struggle throwing the ball to first base, the soft slap is a great tool for directing the ball to that infielder and creating an error. With a slapper at the plate and a fast runner on first base who is a threat to steal, some teams will be forced to play the shortstop closer to second base to cover on the steal. This defense presents a good opportunity for a soft slap to shortstop. The shortstop will have a difficult time making a play if she has to charge and move toward third to field the ball.

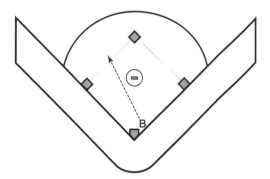

Figure 2.12 Placement for the soft slap.

Drill Progression

Just as with the drag bunt, players should begin learning the soft slap by doing stationary drills so they can learn proper upper-body mechanics. Taking breaks between sets on stationary drills keeps slappers fresh so they do not practice bad mechanics. They can then progress to moving through the batter's box while slapping. Finally, they can put it all together, including sprinting to first base.

SOFT SLAP CONTACT

Purpose   This drill helps the slapper learn the correct path of the hands and barrel to the ball, the proper position of the hands and barrel at contact, and how to create a barrel angle to slap to the 5-6 hole. The slapper also learns proper balance at contact.

Execution   Set up a tee and position it so that the slapper contacts the ball at a location even with or just slightly in front of her left foot. Set up two cones in the field to mark the 5-6 hole. To learn proper position at contact, the slapper starts in a crossed-over position and executes the hand mechanics of the soft slap while stationary. From this position, the slapper hits the ball off a batting tee, making sure that she stops the barrel at contact (see figure 2.13). The slapper's target should always be the 5-6 hole. The slapper should do one set of 10 repetitions and then take a short break, followed by another set of 10 repetitions.

Figure 2.13   Drill in action.

Coaching Points   Make sure that the soft slaps are being hit in the direction of the 5-6 hole. When working in the batting cage, the coach may need to help the slapper find a visual target simulating where the 5-6 hole would be. If the tee is set up correctly (positioned even with the slapper's left foot), but the slapper is not hitting the ball in the proper location, it should be easy to see the adjustment that is needed and to create a barrel angle that will achieve the desired result. This drill also provides a great checkpoint for footwork: parallel lines, toes pointed toward a spot slightly left of the pitcher, nose over the toes, weight on the ball of the left foot, and right heel off the ground.

SOFT SLAP CONTACT AND FOOTWORK

Purpose   After the slapper has learned proper hand mechanics and balance at contact for the soft slap, she is ready to add the crossover step to her drill work. This drill teaches proper timing for the soft slap, including when to start the crossover step so that the slapper makes contact with the ball at the same time that her left foot lands.

Execution   Still working off a batting tee (as with the Soft Slap Contact drill), the slapper now begins in her natural batting stance; she executes the crossover step, performs a short pepper swing to make contact, and jogs a few steps toward the pitcher after contact. The slapper completes two sets of 10 repetitions with a break between sets. Her keys are the same as in the previous drill, but now she is executing while moving through the ball.

Coaching Points   In this drill, slappers sometimes fail to keep their upper body down and over the contact area. The slapper must maintain this posture through contact in order to stay in and cover the outside and low pitch. She also needs to keep her feet moving and maintain good momentum during and after contact.

SOFT SLAP—PUT IT ALL TOGETHER

Purpose   Finally, the slapper is ready to put it all together and run to first base after contact. This drill helps the slapper understand how all of the elements of the soft slap (timing of crossover, contact point, barrel angle, and so on) must work together, and it allows the slapper to determine if she lacks proficiency in any element. A slapper should not practice this drill until she can execute the fundamentals for the two previous drills.

Execution   The best strategy is to start this drill using a pitching machine or front toss so that the slapper can continue to focus on good mechanics. The slapper begins from a regular batting stance position and executes the soft slap, running it out through first base. The drill can be done with a group of slappers lined up at home plate. After the first slapper takes her hit, the next slapper steps up to the plate while the first slapper jogs back to get in line to wait for her next turn. The drill continues until each slapper has completed 5 to 10 repetitions. After the slapper is executing properly off of front toss or a pitching machine, she is ready to perform the soft slap off a live pitcher.

Coaching Points   Make sure the slapper's timing is good (timing between the left foot landing and the contact with the ball) because this is the key to keeping her feet moving at contact and into her sprint to first base. If mechanics break down at this stage, the slapper should go back to drill 2 in the progression and continue working until she is ready to advance.

TOSS AND CATCH

Purpose In this drill, the slapper learns proper footwork and where to make contact with the ball. She also learns to let the ball travel deep in the zone in order to slap to the left side of the infield. This is a great beginning drill for learning the contact point and for keeping a good pace or momentum through and after contact.

Execution The slapper stands in the batter's box with a fielder's glove on her left hand (and no bat; figure 2.14*a*). A partner acts as the pitcher and tosses a ball from approximately 15 feet (4.5 m) away. The slapper crosses over and catches the ball in the glove, making sure that the glove is even with the left foot at the time of the catch (figure 2.14*b*). She keeps her feet moving for a few steps after the catch. The slapper completes one set of 10 repetitions.

Figure 2.14 Slapper's *(a)* starting position and *(b)* position at the catch.

Coaching Points Make sure the slapper doesn't reach out with her glove and catch the ball too far in front of her left foot. One of the goals for this drill is to let the ball travel deep to create a barrel angle that will direct the ball to the 5-6 hole. The slapper needs to develop a good understanding of the contact point necessary to create this barrel angle. Make sure the slapper continues moving her feet after the catch.

WALL SWING

Purpose   This drill teaches the slapper to keep her hands inside on the swing and to keep the barrel close to her body until her hands are even with her right hip.

Execution   The slapper stands facing a net, fence, or other wall-like barrier. She should stand close enough to the wall so that the end of the bat touches the wall while the knob is even with her right hip (see figure 2.15). Then, the slapper chokes up on the bat at least halfway up the bat grip material. She should then practice swinging through (without a ball toss or pitch) without hitting the net or other barrier. The slapper performs two sets of 10 repetitions.

Coaching Points   Make sure the slapper doesn't open her front shoulder and pull out in order to avoid hitting the net; the emphasis is on moving the hands in a straight path toward the pitcher.

Figure 2.15   Proper stance near the barrier.

HARD SLAP

When using the hard slap, the slapper's goal is to hit the ball hard so that the defense isn't able to play shallow to defend the bunt and soft slap. A slapper who is a triple threat—meaning she is able to drag bunt, soft slap, and hard slap with power or hit away—is the most difficult player to defend in softball. If the defense plays shallow to defend the drag bunt and soft slap, the batter can burn them with the hard slap. If they play normal depth to defend the hard slap, she can take advantage of their positioning by dropping a bunt or soft slap.

Sarah Fekete, a former University of Tennessee All-American and one of the best slappers in the game, developed all three of these skills over the course of her career. When speaking to young slappers, she has described the advantage of being a triple threat as follows: "By my senior year, I felt like the defense never got me out . . . I got myself out. They always gave me something to go to, whether it was my bunt, soft slap, or hard slap. If I executed the right skill for the defense they were playing, I knew I would get on base. If I didn't get on base, it was because I hadn't done my job."

Technique

Three hitting options exist for the hard slap: hit the ball hard on the ground in an infield gap, hit a line drive, or drive the ball over the outfield when they are playing shallow. The swing mechanics are the same for all three types of hits and are consistent with soft slap mechanics from ready position to contact. The swing plane is still level. To hit the hard ground ball, the slapper aims for the top half of the ball. To hit the line drive, she aims for the middle of the ball. To hit a deep fly ball, she needs to hit slightly under the middle of the ball.

The point where things change is at contact. With the hard slap, the batter doesn't stop the barrel at contact. Rather, she finishes the swing, keeping the barrel long in the hitting zone (see figure 2.16). To finish and follow through with the swing, the slapper must slow her feet down at contact. She will need to do this in order to maintain balance through the swing and to generate

Figure 2.16 *(a)* The contact, *(b)* the bat position just after contact, and *(c)* the follow through.

the extra power to hit the ball hard. Because she is slowing down somewhat to generate more power, her posture will also be more balanced rather than leaning forward in a nose-over-toes position.

Placement and Strategy

If the infield defense plays in to defend the drag bunt or soft slap, this opens up opportunities for the slapper to drive the ball hard past the infielders (see figure 2.17a). One of the few times that a slapper will try not to hit the ball into the 5-6 hole is when the shortstop is shaded into that hole. In that situation, a hard ground ball up the middle is a great strategy (figure 2.17b). With runners in scoring position, the slapper may look to drive the ball somewhere in the outfield and attempt to hit it hard in a gap. If the outfield defense plays shallow, the slapper can use a hard slap and try to drive the ball over or through the outfield (figure 2.17c). Placement is more difficult to control when using the hard slap. However, to take advantage of a shallow defense, the most important thing is to hit the ball hard.

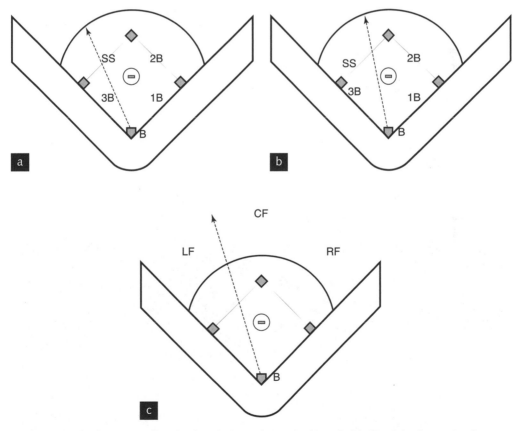

Figure 2.17 Placement for the hard slap when (a) the infield plays shallow, (b) the shortstop plays in the 5-6 hole, or (c) the outfield plays shallow.

Another factor that plays into the slapper's decision regarding which tool to use is the infield surface. When the infield is hard, a hard slap is a better option than a bunt or soft slap. A hard surface will allow the ball to get through the infield gaps faster. When the infield is soft, a bunt or soft slap is likely the better option. A hard slap will have less chance of getting through the infield if the surface is soft.

Drill Progression

The drill progression is identical to that for the soft slap. The slapper should start with stationary hitting, progress to moving through the batter's box, then finally put it all together and run to first. The only thing that changes from the drills described in the soft slap section is that the batter finishes the swing each time. Emphasize keeping the barrel long in the hitting zone. The slapper needs to keep the barrel on the same plane that she wants the ball to travel on so that she doesn't pull off the ball. She will not get the distance or power she wants if she pulls off the ball and away from the hitting zone.

HARD SLAP CONTACT

Purpose This drill helps the slapper learn the correct path of the hands and barrel to the ball, proper balance at contact, and how to stay long through the ball at contact. The slapper also learns where to make contact on the ball for ground balls, line drives, and fly balls.

Execution Set up a batting tee. Starting in a crossed-over position, the slapper executes the mechanics for the hard slap while stationary. From this position, the slapper hits the ball off the tee, making sure that she keeps her barrel long through the ball after contact (see figure 2.18a). The slapper performs two sets of 10 repetitions, resting between sets.

Figure 2.18 *(a)* Correct technique for keeping the barrel long through the ball and *(b)* incorrect rolling of the wrist.

Coaching Points   Make sure that the slapper keeps her barrel in the hitting zone after contact; she should not roll her wrist and pull off the ball (figure 2.18*b*). This is also referred to as hitting in a long zone, and it will help the slapper generate power. The slapper will be in a more balanced position at contact (rather than the nose over toes position) because the hard slap requires a full finish of the swing.

HARD SLAP CONTACT AND FOOTWORK

Purpose   After the slapper has learned the proper swing mechanics and contact points for the hard slap, she is ready to add the crossover step to her drill work. This drill helps the slapper learn proper timing, including when to start the crossover step so that she makes contact with the ball in a balanced position and is able to drive the ball hard into the outfield.

Execution   Still working off a batting tee (as with the Hard Slap Contact drill), the slapper now begins in her natural batting stance; she executes the crossover step, swings to *and through* contact, and continues jogging for a few steps after contact. The slapper performs two sets of 10 repetitions with a break between sets. Her key is to keep the barrel long through the ball after contact, but now she is executing while moving to and through the ball.

Coaching Points   The slapper must stay down and over the plate on the crossover step and must keep the barrel long through the ball at contact. Even though her body weight is more evenly distributed at contact (rather than nose over toes), she still must be sure that she doesn't pull her front shoulder out and get too tall when she swings. This is a common mistake that results from a slapper trying to swing too hard to generate power. The key to power is to keep the front shoulder in and keep the barrel long in the hitting zone.

HARD SLAP—PUT IT ALL TOGETHER

Purpose   In this drill, the slapper works on performing the hard slap and maintaining momentum after contact to run to first base. The slapper should be able to properly execute the two previous drills before attempting to put it all together.

Execution   A group of slappers line up at home plate. The first slapper steps into the batter's box for her turn. The best strategy is to start this drill using front toss so that the slapper can continue to focus on good mechanics. The slapper takes up her normal batting stance; she performs the hard slap, finishes her swing after contact, and continues to run to first base after she has put the ball in play. The next slapper steps up to home plate while the first batter jogs to the end of the line. The drill continues until each slapper

(continued)

Hard Slap—Put It All Together (continued)

completes 5 to 10 turns. After slappers are executing properly off the tosses, they can move to a pitching machine and then advance to executing the hard slap off a live pitcher.

Coaching Points Make sure the slapper finishes her swing and stays through the ball at contact. A common mistake that slappers make once they are running the play out to first base is to pull in the direction of first base before or as they make contact. Doing this will decrease their ability to hit with power. To help slappers avoid pulling out, a coach can tell the slappers to imagine two or three more balls in front of the one they are hitting and to try to hit each of those imaginary balls. This gives the slapper a visual point of reference for staying long in the hitting zone.

Variation The coach can vary the drill by directing the slapper to hit a ground ball, line drive, or fly ball. The slapper can also work inside and outside pitches by hitting the outside pitches to left and left center and hitting the inside pitches to right and right center. Another option is to work on driving the ball up the middle and back at the pitcher.

HIGH-CHOPPER SLAP

The high-chopper slap results when the infield surface is hard and the slapper is able to get a really high bounce. This type of slap is almost impossible to defend. If the ball bounces high enough, there is nothing the infielder can do but wait for it to come down. And by the time the ball comes down, it is often too late for the fielder to throw the slapper out at first. The field surface plays a large part in the execution of this slap, but slappers can get this result using either the soft or hard slap technique. However, the slapper must make contact with the top half of the ball in order to make the ball bounce as close to home plate as possible. This angle will generate the high bounce on a hard infield surface.

HIGH-CHOP BOUNCE

Purpose In this drill, slappers practice making the ball bounce high. They should use whatever technique helps them generate that high bounce, regardless of whether it's soft slap mechanics, hard slap mechanics, or a combination of both.

Execution A group of slappers line up at home plate. A pitching or protective screen is placed approximately 20 feet (6.1 m) from home plate. The screen should be 8 feet (2.4 m) tall. Either use a pitching machine or throw live to the slappers (figure 2.19). Use regular softballs in order to get realistic bounces. The slapper's goal is to make every slap bounce over the screen. The slappers take turns at-bat until they each complete 5 to 10 repetitions.

Figure 2.19 Drill action.

Coaching Points Some slappers stop the barrel at contact and focus on keeping the barrel on top of the ball. Others swing through but emphasize rolling their wrist at contact over the top half to get the downward angle and high bounce. The best approach to teaching this skill (and sometimes others) is to tell the slapper the desired result—in this case, a high bounce—and then let her naturally find the best way for her to achieve that result. Have your slappers compete to see who can create the highest bounce.

CHAPTER **3**

Baserunning

Baserunning is an important component of high-scoring softball. Although baserunning may not be as glamorous as hitting home runs, good baserunning skills can make the difference in whether a team wins or loses. Runners are often safe or out at a base by a fraction of a second or an inch. Learning to run the bases correctly will tip the scale toward safe rather than out.

To have a high-scoring offense, a team must be aggressive on the bases and must be willing to take risks. Players should err on the side of being overly aggressive rather than being too passive. Off-season workouts and preseason practices are the perfect time to test the limits and to learn to be aggressive on the bases without being reckless. Practice is also the time when habits are formed; therefore, if coaches want their teams to run the bases aggressively, they must insist that their teams practice that way.

AGGRESSIVE BASERUNNING PRINCIPLES

Being a good base runner requires two primary characteristics: effort and thought. Although speed can be improved slightly with good running technique, players have no control over whether they are blessed with God-given speed. However, everyone can control their effort and thought, and by doing so, they can maximize their ability to run the bases effectively within an aggressive philosophy. Some of the best base runners are not fast, and some of the worst base runners are extremely fast. The difference is the amount of effort they devote to this particular skill, along with the thought process that allows them to anticipate situations quicker on the field.

Players Run Until the Defense Stops Them

Here's a common scenario in softball: A player hits the ball through the infield, starts slowing to a jog as she approaches first base—assuming that the hit is only going to result in a single—and then sees the outfielder bobble the ball. Because the base runner has already slowed down, she is not able to advance to second. Or the batter hits a pop fly and jogs out of the box, assuming that the ball will be caught. Then, the ball is dropped, but the runner only gets to first base when she could have easily made it to second. Coaches must consistently tell their players to run until the defense stops them. When the defense forces a player to stop running, the player should then—and only then—return to the last base she crossed. Players always want to be in a position to take the extra base if the defense doesn't field the ball cleanly.

Another advantage of players running until the defense stops them is that the runners can force the defense to make errors. These errors are typically made when defenders rush the play or when they are playing nervous and uptight. If the defense knows that their opponent is aggressive on the bases and will take the extra base if defenders don't get to the ball quickly (and field it cleanly), the defense is more likely to get anxious and hurry the play. This increases the chances of an error.

Players Keep Their Eyes on the Ball

Whenever a player is running the bases, she must keep her eyes on the ball. Players sometimes put their head down or turn their back to the ball as they are returning to a base. When a player does this, she may not see an overthrow as the ball is being relayed back to the pitcher. Her coach, her teammates, and even the fans may be screaming for her to advance a base; but she will not be able to react quickly enough to the situation because she did not see what they saw. As a result, the opportunity is lost.

People respond quicker to information gained through their eyes than to what they hear with their ears. There is no reason for a base runner to take her eyes off the ball, even when she is off the bases. The bases do not move. When returning to first base, the runner will find the base without looking at it for 15 feet! Again, when a defense knows that the opponent is aggressive and anticipating defensive errors, the defense is more prone to make those errors because the defenders are forced to play the game faster.

Players Check the Defense Before Every Pitch

A smart base runner looks to see where the defensive players are positioned before the pitch is thrown. Using this information, the runner is able to make quicker decisions on whether to advance depending on where and how hard the ball is hit. For example, if the right fielder is playing off the line and the ball is hit close to the right-field line, a smart base runner will take off from first base immediately and advance to third without hesitation. This base runner knows that the fielder wasn't positioned close enough to the line to catch the ball or throw all the way to third base in time to throw the runner out. Of course, the base runner's speed factors into this play. A runner with average speed, however, will likely be able to advance to third if she used the prepitch knowledge available to her and reacted immediately.

A base runner on second who checks the outfield positioning may notice that an outfielder is playing deep. If a ball is blooped into shallow outfield, the base runner will be able to quickly make a decision to go on the hit. The runner will have a much better chance to score because she got a quick jump off the base. Base runners need to check the defense every pitch because the defense may change their positioning from pitch to pitch.

Players Use a Hip-to-Lip Arm Movement

A discussion of proper running form and technique could easily take up an entire chapter, but that is not the focus of this book. One helpful tip that is

Figure 3.1 Base runners should (a) keep their elbows tucked in and at 90 degrees and (b) move their hands from their hips to their lips.

easy to remember is "hip to lip." When running the bases, players should have their arms at a 90-degree angle with the elbows close to the body and with the hands directly in front of the elbows (see figure 3.1). From this position, the player pumps her arms by taking the hands from hip to lip. The player must be sure to maintain the 90-degree angle in the arms at all times.

STRATEGIES FOR RUNNING FROM HOME TO FIRST BASE

Assume that the player hits the ball to the infield and there is likely going to be a play at first base. When running out of the box, the player should run in a straight line and maintain that line as she crosses first base (see figure 3.2). Young players are often taught to veer toward foul territory as they cross the base. There is no advantage to this; in fact, there are disadvantages. First, the player who veers into foul territory has created a longer distance to second base if an overthrow occurs at first base. Second, a player in the habit of doing this may start to veer to the right before she touches first base; thus, she takes extra time to hit the base. Remember, the shortest distance between two points is a straight line. Base runners want to be sure they are traveling the shortest distance when possible. To give players an easy cue, a coach can instruct them to run on the foul line and stay on the foul line when they cross first base.

The player should always touch the front half of first base. The umpire determines safe or out based on whether the player touches first base before or

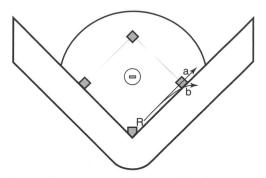

Figure 3.2   Path *a* shows the correct path across first base. Path *b*, the veer, provides no advantage.

after the ball gets to first. If the player touches the middle or backside of first base, she is giving the defense extra time to get the ball to first base. Remember, safe or out calls are determined by fractions of seconds and inches. A player should not, however, shuffle her feet in order to hit the base correctly. This will cost valuable time. To help avoid the need to use a shuffle step, the player should pick up first base with her eyes early on the way from home to first base. Her feet will naturally adjust so that she can maintain good long strides while running.

The player must run hard *through* first base. Immediately after crossing the base, the player should come to a stop as soon as possible. This will enable the player to change direction and be ready to advance to second on an overthrow. Again, the shortest distance between two points is a straight line; stopping early after crossing first base will cut down the distance to second base.

To stop quickly, the player uses a technique known as breaking down. The player widens her base, or feet, and lowers her rear end (see figure 3.3). This will help her maintain balance as she comes to a sudden stop. As the player does this, she should turn her head toward foul territory to look for the possible overthrow. When she can see the overthrow herself rather than rely on the first-base coach for information, the player will be able to respond quicker and make a good decision on whether to advance to second base.

Let's assume that the player is safe at first and the ball was caught cleanly

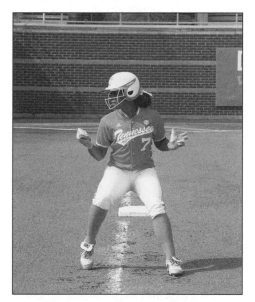

Figure 3.3   Position for breaking down.

by the first-base player. After the runner breaks down and stops, she should return to first base on the foul line. She should turn her head toward the field of play when returning to the base. As long as she is returning directly to first base, she is not a "live" player for the defense to attempt to tag. If she makes an attempt toward second, however, she becomes a live player, and the defense can tag her out when she is off the base.

STRATEGIES FOR RUNNING FROM HOME TO SECOND BASE

Keeping in mind the principles of aggressive baserunning and running until the defense forces a stop, the base runner should be thinking *two bases* anytime the ball is put in play beyond the infield. As the batter leaves the batter's box, she is running hard for second base and will continue to second (and beyond if the play allows her to) until the defense forces her to stop and return to first base. This same aggressive thought process should be used when the runner starts at first or second base.

When a player hits the ball through or over the infield, she should run out of the box in a way that sets her up for making a good, efficient turn at first base to head toward second base. When she touches first, she wants her body squared up to second as much as possible so that she is now running in a straight line to second base. To do this, she must create an angle while running to first that allows her to make a good turn toward second. Too many players run in a straight line to first base and then end up way outside the baseline between first and second, making a very wide, inefficient turn (see figure 3.4). Or they run straight to first base out of the box and then turn toward foul territory in the path of a question mark. Again, players must always remember that the shortest distance between two points is a straight line. So if a player

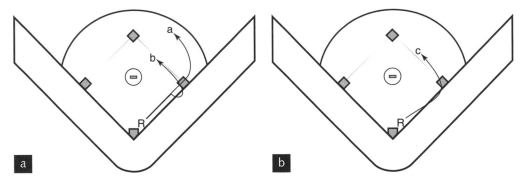

Figure 3.4   (*a*) Path *a* is an inefficient turn and path *b* takes additional time. (*b*) Path *c* is the most efficient baserunning option.

knows that she is going to have to go into foul territory in order to make the turn, she should run straight to that spot out of the box. The player needs to create the angle early out of the box (or early off the base in the case of first or second) so that she is as quick and efficient as possible advancing to the next base.

It does not matter which foot the player uses to touch the base. A player should never slow down or use a shuffle step in order to hit the base with a certain foot. The important thing is that the player touches the inside corner of the base (see figure 3.5). The player should always lean to the left (toward the pitcher's circle) when touching a base. This will help the player maintain good balance and avoid wide turns into the outfield side of the basepaths.

Figure 3.5 Base runner touching the inside corner of the base.

STRATEGIES FOR RUNNING FROM HOME TO THIRD BASE

When the ball is hit to an outfield gap and goes past the outfielders, the batter should be thinking *three bases* and, again, should run until the defense stops her. If playing on an open field and if the ball is hit hard enough, the batter may actually make it all the way around and cross home plate. For purposes of this discussion, however, we will assume that there is an outfield fence enclosing the field. Triples are difficult to come by in fastpitch softball because the fences are typically 200 to 225 feet away. Most balls in the gaps result in doubles, especially if the batter possesses only average speed. However, a faster batter may be able to stretch the hit to a triple, especially on balls hit either down the right-field line or in the right-center gap.

On a ball in the gap, the batter runs out of the batter's box and creates her angle immediately so that she can make a good turn at first base. As she steps on the inside corner of first base, she begins to create her angle to make another good turn at second base. She doesn't have to run straight toward the second-base bag because there likely won't be a close play at second. The main goal is to set herself up for the possibility of getting to third base. The better the angles and turns around first and second base, the less time it will take the runner to cover the bases, and the greater chance she will have to advance to third.

Because triples usually occur on balls hit to right center and down the right-field line, the runner needs to pick up the third-base coach early enough (when she is between first and second base) to see the coach's signal to advance to third base. In most situations, base runners should use their eyes as much as possible to make decisions, rather than rely on the base coach. In this situation, however, the base runner must look for assistance because the ball will be behind her field of vision.

RUNNING FROM FIRST OR SECOND BASE

When a runner begins the play at first or second base, she should use home-to-first running techniques in the following situations: if stealing, if the bunt play is on, or if the ball is put into play in the infield and there is a potential force-out at the base to which she is advancing. If, however, the base runner's teammate (the batter) hits the ball through the infield (and it is not a potential tag-up situation), the runner should use home-to-second running techniques and create a good angle for rounding the next base; she should anticipate advancing two bases instead of just one. Base runners must remember to run until the defense stops them!

LEADOFFS

There is an ongoing debate in softball circles about the type of leadoff that players should use on the bases. Some argue that the rocker positioning (see

figure 3.6) is best, while others subscribe to the starter positioning (see figure 3.7). On our team, we want players to use whichever positioning helps them to be on time off the base. The base runner can leave the base when the ball leaves the pitcher's hand. Therefore, she needs to be sure that she is leaving the base at that time and no later. A runner who is late off the bases is much more vulnerable to a pickoff because she is still moving off the base as the ball is being received by the catcher. A runner who is on time off the base will be balanced and able to get back quickly on a pickoff throw.

Figure 3.6 The rocker leadoff position.

Videotape of base runners reveals that many players who use the rocker position actually start too late and are still on the base when the ball is on its way to home plate. In this case, if the players can make the adjustment to starting their motion earlier, they should continue using the rocker position because it gives the runner extra momentum. If they can't make the adjustment, they should switch to the starter position so that they do not lose time on their leadoff.

With either the rocker or starter positioning, the runner should always have her left foot in contact with the base. The front half of the foot should be in contact with the ground, and the back half should be on the base (see figure 3.8). The runner uses the base to push off, much like a starter's block in track. The runner should position her foot on the portion of the base that is closest to the outfield so that she is farthest from a potential pickoff throw by the catcher.

Figure 3.7   The starter leadoff position.

Figure 3.8   Proper foot position on a base.

Leads From First Base

From first base, the runner takes a three-step lead, squaring up to the plate on her third step (see figure 3.9 on page 58). The runner must be balanced when she squares up and not leaning toward second base. The distance between home and first is 60 feet—not a very long throw for a catcher attempting a pickoff. A leaning, off-balance runner is an easy target for a pickoff. If the runner takes more than three steps, she will likely be too far off the base and will be vulnerable to a pickoff. The distance of the leadoff may change based on where the first-base player is positioned. If the first-base player is playing close to the base, the runner may have to cut down the distance of her leadoff, and vice versa.

If the runner uses the rocker positioning on the base, her first step with her right foot is step 1, the step with her left foot is step 2, and the last step with

Figure 3.9 Runner squaring up to the plate on a leadoff.

her right foot is step 3; she squares her shoulders to the plate on this third step. If the runner uses the starter positioning with her left foot on the base and her right foot in front of the base, the right foot being placed in front at the start counts as the first step. So, the player takes only two additional steps. The second step is with her left foot, and the third step is with her right foot; she squares her shoulders to the plate on this third step. The key is that the runner is no more than three steps off first base and that her feet are in a position to square up to home on the third step.

Leads From Second Base

Regarding placement of the foot on the base and starting positioning, the techniques used at first base apply to leads from second as well. However, the runner now takes a five-step lead. She can afford to do this because the distance from home to second base is 84 feet 10 inches, thus making the catcher's pickoff throw longer. A runner at second base is in scoring position and should be thinking *score* on any base hit. We tell our runners to take a "scoring lead." In other words, when taking their lead, they will begin to create the angle for making a good turn at third base. The exceptions to this are the same as at first base—the runner should always run in a straight line to the next base when stealing or if the bunt play is on.

Leads From Third Base

Foot placement and starting positioning remain consistent when the runner is starting at third base. However, some differences exist in the strategy used at third. Unless the suicide squeeze play is on, the player should take a more passive lead. The worst thing that can happen at third is for a runner to be doubled off on a line drive because she was being too aggressive with her leadoff. The runner will score easily on almost every type of base hit to the outfield, so there is no reason to fire off the base too fast or too far and run into a line-drive double play. The runner must also be in position to tag up and score on a ball hit in the air to the outfield. Runners who lead off aggressively often cannot get back in time to tag, and they lose an opportunity to score a run.

Another key at third is to make sure the runner leads off in foul territory (see figure 3.10). If she is struck by a batted ball in foul territory, the ball is dead, and she returns to the base. If, however, she is struck in fair territory, she is automatically out. There is no need to lead off on or inside the baseline and run the risk of being struck by a fair ball. The runner at third base should never lead off beyond the positioning of the third-base player. Doing so will make the runner extremely vulnerable to being picked off by the catcher. This is especially true when a left-handed batter is in the batter's box.

Figure 3.10   The runner on third base takes a passive lead into foul territory.

STEALING

Stealing bases is a key part of aggressive baserunning. Obviously, speed is a very important element of success in stealing. However, a fast runner can increase her chance of stealing safely by using good running technique and timing (as discussed previously). She must be sure to leave the base as the ball leaves the pitcher's hand—and not a fraction of a second later.

Developing great timing will likely require the use of video, especially if the runner uses the rocker positioning. The advantage of the rocker positioning is that, if the runner's timing is good, her body is already in motion as the ball leaves the pitcher's hand. The challenge with the rocker is developing the ability to start the feet in motion at the right time, because this must happen before the pitcher actually releases the ball.

Good base runners are also able to adjust to the different deliveries of pitchers. Some pitchers have a fast arm motion; others are much slower. Good base runners will study the pitcher during the warm-up pitches between innings and will get her timing down. Knowing when to start can be the difference between being safe or out in a close play on a steal attempt.

Straight Steals of Second or Third Base

When stealing, the base runner should run in a straight line to the base. Typically, the runner will slide to the side of the base that is farthest away from the ball. However, the runner should not slide around a fielder or slide by the base and reach back with a hand. When using these methods, runners take more time to reach the base, and time is critical in stealing bases.

The runner must also decide whether to slide headfirst or feetfirst. Each method has both pros and cons. Base runners should not slide headfirst into home plate because of the potential for a collision with the catcher's shin guards—and the risk of a head or neck injury. At second and third base, however, the *quickest* way to reach the base is to slide headfirst; the runner slides with her hands outstretched, and she touches the base first with her hand. If the runner is attempting to disrupt the defensive player making a play on her (break up a double play or get between the fielder and a thrown ball), the feetfirst slide may be the better choice.

Stealing on Balls in the Dirt and on Changeups

Teams should work on being ready to steal on pitches in the dirt and on changeups. The base runners should try to read the pitch angle as early as possible after the pitcher releases the ball. They should steal on any ball they believe is going to bounce in the dirt before it reaches the catcher. The runners may be tipped off that the ball is going in the dirt by watching to see if the catcher drops to her knees early to prepare to block the ball in the dirt. They also should try to read the changeup (either by a clue from the pitcher or as soon as possible after release) and attempt to steal when they see it.

The leadoff is a very important part of this skill. Leads must be on time but not so explosive that the runner has to stop, read the pitch or angle, and then restart. Once the runner stops, she has lost the opportunity because it takes too long to get the body restarted. The key here is to take a jogging lead. This enables the runner to maintain momentum and transfer to a sprint when she sees the steal opportunity. She is also able to change direction and return to the base if the opportunity for a steal is not there.

A pitcher who throws a lot of drop balls or changeups can create a lot of opportunities for the opponent to steal bases. When the defense knows that the offense is looking for any chance to run, the defense tends to make mistakes. An anxious catcher may take her eye off the ball because she is worried about the runner. She may fail to frame pitches because of the threat of a steal, thus costing her pitcher strike calls. A pitcher may be worried about throwing a ball in the dirt with a runner on base and may end up leaving the pitch up in the zone for the hitter to crush. Aggressive baserunning can result in a defense playing anxious—and when the defense gets anxious, mistakes occur.

Delayed Steal

The delayed steal is a great play to use to demoralize a defense. Earlier in the chapter, we discussed running through first base on an infield hit and staying on a straight line (the foul line) after crossing the bag. The delayed steal after a safe call at first is set up by two things: (1) the shortstop and second-base player leaving second base unoccupied and not paying attention to the runner who has just crossed first safely, and (2) the nature of the base runner's return to first base.

To execute the delayed steal, the runner turns to her *left* after she crosses first base and *walks* back to first base along the foul line, looking immediately to see if the shortstop and second-base player have vacated second base and are not paying attention to her. The runner must walk and take her time on her return to first, allowing the play to develop. Middle infielders often walk back to their positions with their head down after an infield hit. If the base runner sees that the middle infielders are too far away from second base and are not paying attention, the runner should take off for second base. *Even if the ball is in the pitcher's circle* when the runner breaks for second, this play is legal as long as the runner has not stopped on first base. Once the runner stops at first, she must stay there; otherwise, she will be called out for being off the base after the ball was returned to the pitcher's circle.

Another type of delayed steal (which is more common) is to steal off the catcher's throw back to the pitcher after a pitch. This play will be successful if these circumstances are present: (1) The catcher is getting lazy with her throws back to the pitcher and is not keeping the runners from taking big leads; (2) the pitcher is putting her head down or turning away from the runner when receiving the ball back from the catcher; and (3) the runner lulls the pitcher and catcher into thinking that she is not a threat to run, and she times her break well when she sees the opportunity.

TAGGING UP

Players are often confused about when to tag up on a fly ball and when not to. Here's a simple rule that takes care of most fly-ball situations: Runners should tag up *only* when they will advance on the catch. Otherwise, the base runner should get off the base far enough to sprint back safely if the ball is caught or to advance if the ball is dropped. The only exception to this rule is that base runners must tag up on all foul balls, because the runners can't advance on a dropped foul ball anyway.

Coaches must instruct their players regarding what the players should do on the tough plays where an outfielder is running away from the infield and the ball may or may not be caught. Some coaches want to take a chance that the outfielder won't make the play; these coaches instruct their runners to move on the hit. With this strategy, the goal is for the runners to advance extra bases if the ball isn't caught. The downside to this philosophy is that the runners may end up having to go back to their original base if the ball is caught. Other coaches may want their runners to tag up and be sure of advancing at least one base if the ball is caught. The downside here is that the runners likely won't advance more than one base if the ball isn't caught. Whether the game is played on an open field or a field with an outfield fence will play a key role in the strategy used.

To determine when to leave the base, runners should watch the catch rather than rely on the coach to tell them when to leave. They will react quicker to information processed with their eyes than to information they hear with their ears. At third base, the coach will tell the runner either "yes" or "no" when the ball is in the air. If the player hears "yes," she watches the catch and breaks for home as soon as the ball hits the fielder's glove. If the player hears "no," she watches the catch and then breaks off third base hard as if she is going to try to score (fakes going home); she tries to draw a throw—and possibly an overthrow—by the defense. She does not attempt to go on the catch but is ready to score if the defense makes a mistake.

At times, a coach may prefer to instruct the player when to leave the base on a tag-up play. If a particular base runner tends to leave early, even when the defense doesn't have a chance to throw her out, the coach may want to have the runner leave on the coach's command. In certain game situations, the coach may prefer to take responsibility for that decision and not risk a player leaving the base too early and being called out.

Whenever possible, a base runner should try to run in the throwing lane between the two defensive players who are trying to throw and catch on the play (see figure 3.11). For example, when a runner is tagging at third on a fly ball on or near the left-field line, the runner should stay in the line between the left fielder and the catcher when attempting to score. If a base runner is hit with a thrown ball, the ball is still live, and there is no negative effect on the offensive team. If the base runner can run in the throwing lane and inter-fere with the defense's ability to make a play, she will have a better chance of reaching the next base successfully. She may also cause an errant throw and create an opportunity to advance extra bases.

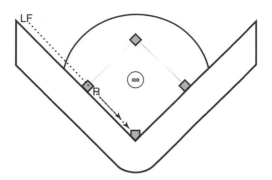

Figure 3.11 A base runner should try to stay in the throwing lane.

WHEN TO USE THE BASE COACH

As crazy as it may sound, we like our players to use the base coaches as little as possible. Obviously, players need to rely on the base coaches when they cannot see the ball behind them or cannot see fielders covering bases out of their vision (e.g., pickoff plays). The best base runners trust their eyes, know their speed, know their strengths and weaknesses, and use their instincts. In practice, we run many live drills without base coaches. This forces the base runners to think—before the pitch—about where the defense is playing and the relative strength of the defenders' arms. When the ball is put into play, the runners are forced to make quick decisions using all of the information available: defensive positioning before the pitch, how hard the ball is hit, where the ball is hit on the field, and so on. The quicker the runners can make their reads and react, the more likely they are to advance extra bases and to take advantage of opportunities the defense gives them.

Base runners generally make very good decisions when they think ahead of the play and use all of the information they have. By no means are we suggesting that base coaches are not important or should not be used in a game. The coach manages the game and may not want a runner to take a chance on the bases at a particular point in the game, even if the runner believes she can advance safely. But instinctive base runners are better and more aggressive, and base runners become instinctive only when forced to rely on themselves to make good decisions.

Remember, in practice and even in games early in the season, base runners can test their limits and find that line between aggressiveness and recklessness. The team may run themselves out of a few innings while doing so, but in the long run, they will be better for it. Late in the season, an extra base by an aggressive base runner may be the thing that allows the team to advance during the postseason or even win a championship.

BASERUNNING DRILLS

Teams should work on baserunning in each of their practices. Coaches often neglect this aspect of the game. Or they assume that some players are good base runners instinctively and other players are not—and that players cannot do much to improve these skills. However, baserunning skills *can* be improved. The more the players are put into baserunning situations, the better they will be at both baserunning technique and decision making. Not everyone is blessed with great speed, but everyone can be a great base runner.

Baserunning can be practiced in many ways. When the team is working on team defense, the players not currently playing defense can run bases; a coach should be responsible for watching and instructing the baserunning group. During live batting practice, players can practice leads, create angles, read the defense, and make good decisions. Intrasquad scrimmages provide a great opportunity for players to work on baserunning. The key is that players are always accountable for their baserunning. The coaching staff should consistently emphasize the importance of baserunning in the team's offensive philosophy. Baserunning can also be practiced using specific drills. Following are several drills that incorporate the keys discussed in this chapter.

HOME TO FIRST WITH BREAKDOWNS

Purpose   In this drill, the base runner learns the proper technique for running from home to first as quickly and efficiently as possible. She also works on breaking down in a way that allows her to advance to second on an overthrow.

Execution   A group of at least five players line up behind home plate. The first player starts in the batter's box and takes a full swing with the bat. (No ball is used.) She runs through first base and touches the front half of the base. After crossing the base, the player stops by breaking down—that is, by widening her base and lowering her rear. Place cones approximately 10 feet (3 m) beyond first base to represent the point where the player should stop. In other words, the base runner must break down before reaching this point. Another option is to have a coach stand in place of the cones, forcing the player to break down before running into the coach. After her turn, each player jogs back to home to wait for her next turn. Each player should do five repetitions.

Coaching Points   Make sure the player doesn't stutter-step or shuffle her feet in order to hit the front of the bag, because this will take more time. If the player finds the front of the bag with her eyes early out of the batter's box, the feet have a way of automatically adjusting so that she never has to break stride in order to hit the bag properly. Instruct players to run on the balls of their feet and to keep their arms at a 90-degree angle, with the elbows close to the body. The players should move their hands from hip to lip. These tips will help increase the base runner's speed.

HOME TO SECOND WITH CONES

Purpose   This drill helps the player learn how to create an angle before she reaches first base so that her turn to second base is efficient. When the player hits first base, she wants her chest square to second base so that she is able to run in a fairly straight line to second. This helps her avoid veering wide and going out into the basepath toward shallow right field.

Execution   Set up a cone outside the first-base line to mark the angle of the base runner's turn. Then set another cone approximately 8 to 10 feet (2.4 to 3.0 m) past first base (toward second base) and about 4 to 5 feet (122 to 152 cm) to the right-field side of the line between first and second base (see figure 3.12). The second cone represents the boundary for the player's turn. After rounding first base, she cannot run outside of this cone on

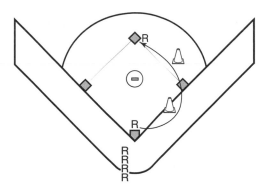

Figure 3.12   Cone setup and running path.

the way to second. A group of five or more players line up behind home plate. The first player starts in the batter's box and takes a full swing with the bat. (No ball is used.) She runs toward the cone and then runs outside of the cone to set her angle for the turn at first base. As the player hits the inside corner of the first-base bag, she leans toward the pitcher's mound and continues in as straight a line as possible to second base. After her turn, each player jogs back to home to wait for her next turn. Each player completes five repetitions.

Coaching Points   Make sure the player runs in a straight line from the batter's box to the first cone; some players tend to follow the foul line for a distance and then veer right and around the cone. Remember, the shortest distance between two points is a straight line. Remind the player that it doesn't matter which foot touches the bag. The key is to touch the corner of the bag closest to the pitcher's mound with either foot and to lean in that direction. This helps the runner maintain a tight and efficient path toward second base.

RUNNERS AT HOME, FIRST, AND THIRD

Purpose In this combination drill, the team can work on running through first base and breaking down; leading off from first and running from first to third, creating proper angles and turns; and leading off from third and returning to tag up and advance to home.

Execution This drill starts with small groups of runners at home, first base, and third base. One person at each base participates in each drill repetition. A player stands in the pitcher's circle (with no ball) and performs a pitching motion so that the runners can time their leads. On the pitcher's motion, the following things happen simultaneously (see figure 3.13):

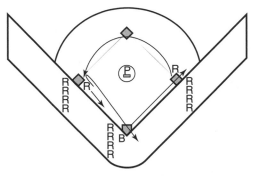

Figure 3.13 Runner movements.

- The runner at home uses a shadow swing, runs straight through first, and then breaks down.

- The runner at first leads off on the motion, then runs from first to third on the swing, setting a good angle and making a good turn at second. (The runner can slide or use a stutter stop at third.)

- The runner at third leads off on the motion, goes back and tags on the swing, watches an imaginary catch in the outfield, and then advances to home.

The next runners in line at each base step up for the next repetition of the drill. The runners who just completed a turn get in line at the base that they advanced to. The drill continues until every player has, at minimum, a chance to run from every base, but it can continue long enough for all players to get three to four repetitions from every base.

Coaching Points Make sure the timing is good on the leadoffs at first base. Cones can be set up before and after second base to give the runner guidance for creating an angle and to help her avoid running too wide outside the basepath after crossing second base. At third base, make sure the runner uses starter footwork when she returns to tag up—rather than rocker footwork—so that she will be as close to home as possible. This will enable her to advance more quickly when the imaginary ball is caught in the outfield.

LEADOFF DRILL

Purpose   This drill allows base runners to practice executing proper leadoffs from all of the bases.

Execution   Small groups of runners are at first, second, and third base. One person at each base participates in a drill repetition. A pitcher or coach is in the pitcher's circle performing a pitching motion or actually pitching a ball to a catcher at home (no batter). As the pitcher releases the ball, each base runner takes her leadoff from the base, remembering that the distance and pace of the lead will vary depending on the base she occupies. The coach can have the base runners do one of two things:

- Square up to the plate (except for the runner at third, who stops her lead by squaring up toward the pitcher) and return to the base as if the ball was not put in play.

- Square up momentarily, then continue on to the next base as if the ball was put in play or got past the catcher.

After this repetition, the players on base get in line at the next base. The drill repeats until all players have at least one repetition from each base or until the coach determines everyone has performed enough correct repetitions.

Coaching Points   Make sure the runners are leaving the bases on time. At third base, runners must take a more passive lead. The runners must be balanced when they stop to square up so that they can return to the base quickly in case of a pickoff attempt.

TWO-MACHINE DRILL

Purpose   This drill helps a base runner learn to read the height and angle of the ball early and to make quick decisions about whether to advance to the next base or tag up in anticipation of a catch. (The drill also allows the team to work on several defensive skills: communication on fly balls, the cut-and-relay play, and putting tags on base runners.)

Execution   Set up two pitching machines close together in the home plate area. One pitching machine is set to loft a shallow fly ball into right center, and the other is set to send a deep fly ball to right center. The following defensive players set up in proper position: right fielder, center fielder, second-base player, shortstop, and third-base player. Base runners set up at first and second base. A coach operates each machine. Before each repetition the coaches decide who will feed the ball into which machine. Both act as if they are placing a ball in the machine, but only one ball is actually put in play.

The runner at second reacts to the ball shot into the outfield and must choose the best course of action. On a shallow fly ball, she should stay off the base and then run on (if the ball isn't caught) or return to second (if the ball is caught). On a deep fly ball, she should tag up and advance to third on the catch. The runner at first also works on reading the ball and trying to make quick decisions, but she must also read the base runner ahead. The defensive players play out the ball. On the deep fly ball, the center and right fielders communicate about who is going to catch the ball, and the second-base player lines up to be the relay person on the throw to second or third base. On the shallow fly ball, the two outfielders must communicate with the second-base player about who is going to catch the ball and who is going to back up the play; the shortstop covers second base. The drill continues until the players have continued several correct repetitions.

Coaching Points   Make sure the runners are following one simple rule: A runner should tag up only when she will advance to the next base on the catch; otherwise, she should get off the base as far as she can while still being able to sprint back to the base and beat a throw if the ball is caught.

CHAPTER 4

Hitting for Average

This chapter and the next one outline skills and drills associated with players who hit for average and those who hit for power. Coaches would like to have all of their players do both, and every player would like to be able to hit for power and average. In reality, very few players can be a threat to do both. As evidence of this, baseball has not had a triple crown winner in over 30 years. The reason is simple—each style of hitting requires certain physical skills, as well as specific preparation skills.

This chapter covers hitting for average. The chapter outlines the characteristics—both mental and physical—that prepare a batter to hit for a high batting average and also a high on-base percentage. These players are very valuable to an offense. This chapter also includes specific drills to assist players in becoming high-average hitters.

CHARACTERISTICS OF HIGH-AVERAGE HITTERS

When people think of players who hit for average, the following types of hitters come to mind: contact hitter, gap hitter, and situational hitter. These hitters usually possess the following mental characteristics:

- They are students of the game.
- They study opposing pitchers and defenses.
- They are strong mentally.
- They have an offensive game plan.
- They have the ability to adjust within an at-bat.
- They play "smarter not harder."
- They understand the importance of a good on-base percentage.

In addition, high-average hitters usually possess most of the following physical traits:

- Good eyesight
- Good eye–hand coordination
- Solid hitting fundamentals
- Ability to work the count and go deep in the count
- Ability to hit to all fields
- Better-than-average speed and baserunning skills
- A short compact swing

We ask our hitters to provide written goals each month, and then we create an offensive practice plan designed to help the hitters achieve their goals. The goals and practice plan are more detailed for the situational hitters because these hitters need to correctly execute several offensive skills to hit for a high average. Figure 4.1 provides an example of a goal sheet, and figure 4.2 on page 72 provides a sample practice plan.

Most high-average hitters realize that they do not possess some of the physical skills that long-ball hitters possess. They also know that if they are going to be successful, they must understand the game and play the game one pitch at a time. Most important, they need to know all the offensive situations and how they can perfect their approach to each. Being a student of the game of hitting requires a detailed knowledge of pitchers. Hitters need to know the pitchers' strengths and weaknesses, what the pitchers' goals are, and what pitchers tend to throw in certain situations.

Good hitters love to hit. They will take as many cuts in practice as the coach allows. They come early and stay late. They hone their game through hours of repetitive drills and even more time watching video or studying scouting reports. They always want to know how to get better. The best hitters are always pursuing excellence.

Figure 4.1 Sample Goal Sheet

Player's name _____ Month _____

1. Think of three specific areas to work on and emphasize this month. Write them in the form of goals.
2. State a specific action plan for reaching each goal and for preparing to achieve maximum performance.

Three to win	Personal goals	Plan of action
Fitness		
Skill		
Attitude		

I commit myself to strive to the best of my ability to reach the goals I have set for myself and my team this month.

Player's initials _____

From R. Weekly and K. Weekly, 2012, *High-scoring softball* (Champaign, IL: Human Kinetics).

Figure 4.2   Sample Offensive Practice Plan

Date_____

OBJECTIVES

Increase bat speed and work on proper movement of the hands to the ball.

Emphasize palm-up and palm-down position at contact and staying long through the ball.

ACTION PLAN

Step 1 (3:10–3:20 p.m.)

Measure each player's bat speed.

Step 2 (3:20–3:35 p.m.)

Watch a prepared video showing the proper swing path, hand positions at contact, extension, and follow-through. Make certain the players understand exactly what you want as a coach. Demonstrate the swing phase.

Step 3 (3:35–3:40 p.m.)

Set up and explain circuits (see appendices A and B) that emphasize the skills you are teaching:

- High Tee (placed at the contact point; working on correct hand path)
- High tee swing to contact, then pause, checking hands (working on proper hand position at contact)
- Triple Tee (working on staying long through the ball)
- Hitting Tube (working on bat speed and follow-through)
- Woofin Stix (working on bat speed)

Step 4 (3:40–4:15 p.m.)

Work with players and give feedback during circuit training.

Step 5 (3:40–4:15 p.m.)

Videotape players during circuit training.

Step 6

Provide detailed evaluation and instruction to individual players after practice.

High-average hitters often select barrel bats because of the larger contact zone. Most of the good hitters in this category use a bat that is lighter than normal so that they will have good bat control in any situation. They have a very good work ethic, and they know that they must be able to do well in all facets of the short game. They also need to be proficient in using the whole field to their advantage. This skill requires a detailed knowledge of hitting fundamentals, positioning in the batter's box, and all three contact zones.

ON-BASE PERCENTAGE, PITCH RECOGNITION, AND PITCH SELECTION

Hitters striving for a high batting average realize early in their careers that the most important statistic for them is their on-base percentage. To improve this percentage, the first skills they need to master are pitch recognition and pitch selection. On one of our trips to the Women's College World Series, we encountered an opponent whose first four hitters had over 50 bases on balls each. Each of these players had an on-base percentage of .500 or better. This team had only played 56 games before the playoffs. Facing hitters with these kinds of numbers was a challenge for our pitching staff.

This opposing team did not swing until they got their pitch or had two strikes. Even with two strikes, they fouled off the pitches that were close until they got the pitch they wanted. This strategy puts tremendous pressure on the pitcher, who must get ahead in the count and must make every pitch count. We prevailed in the game because we outhit the team, but our pitcher was mentally exhausted after the game. Before this game, we had talked about pitch recognition, but after this game we made it a priority for our offense.

The top hitters on every team already know the value of pitch recognition and pitch selection. For a team to be better offensively, the coaches must stress pitch recognition and pitch selection on a daily basis. A lot of hitters don't even know what "their pitch" is, and many hitters who struggle (and do not have a good average) will swing at anything.

The first thing that players need to do is get their eyes checked. Some players struggle as hitters for years because they cannot see the ball well. Being prescribed glasses or contacts can change a hitter overnight. Glasses or contacts can help the batter see the ball quicker and track it longer. The eye doctor should also test for the dominant eye. When the player has determined her dominant eye, she can also improve her ability to see the ball by changing her stance in the box. For instance, if a right-handed batter's dominant eye is the right eye, she can open up slightly, giving herself a better opportunity to track the ball.

It has been estimated that a pitch thrown 62 mph from 43 feet gets to the batter in .04 seconds. Some studies show slightly different times, but all are within split seconds. Regardless, players need great eyesight and great eye–hand coordination to recognize the pitch and make a hitting decision. Fastpitch softball is a tough game. Hitting the pitch is even tougher. Great hitters see the ball well, and they have taught themselves to recognize the pitch in an instant and make their decision in split seconds. This ability is a learned skill. To become top hitters, players must be students of the game, and they must have goals, a practice plan, and a drive to be the best.

FOCUS DRILLS

These drills are designed to help batters see the ball better. A hitter striving to maintain a high batting average must see the ball well. Hitting requires great visual skills. Simply said, if the batter can't see the ball, she can't hit it. Learning to see the ball well starts in the dugout. The great hitters study the pitcher and learn how to "match motion with the pitcher." They learn the pitcher's release point, and they focus on the ball as it leaves the pitcher's hand. They then track the ball to the contact zone. Great hitters learn to focus and track early in their careers. The following drills can help hitters focus on and track a pitch.

SMALL BAT AND BALL-SIDE TOSS

Purpose   This drill improves a batter's focus because the bat and ball are both much smaller than those normally used in a game.

Execution   For this drill, use a small thin bat and baseballs. (Golf-ball-size Wiffle balls can also be used. A catch net may be useful too.) The batter starts in the batter's box. The coach stands in front and at a 45-degree angle to the left of a right-handed batter (or at a 45-degree angle to the right of a left-handed batter; figure 4.3). The coach tosses the balls at a 45-degree angle to the hitting zones. The coach can toss the balls high, low, or in any

Figure 4.3   Batting with a small bat.

area of the contact zone. The batter uses the small bat and works on tracking the smaller ball. The batter completes three sets of 10 repetitions, stressing proper fundamentals on each repetition.

Coaching Points   Make sure the players do not sacrifice their hitting fundamentals to hit the smaller ball.

Variation   A team without a small bat can use a thin metal bat, or they can substitute a 32-inch broomstick for the bat. Other options for performing the drill include having the coach toss from the front or even from behind the batter so that the batter has to pick up the pitch as it enters her peripheral vision. Another option is to use two different colored Wiffle balls. In this version, the coach tosses both balls into the contact zone and calls out a color. The batter must identify and hit the ball of the correct color.

QUICK TOSS

Purpose   This drill enhances a batter's focus and bat speed. The player must be totally focused to successfully complete this drill. An added benefit is that this drill exercises fast-twitch muscles in the arms.

Execution   The coach tosses the ball to the batter from a position to the side or directly in front of the batter. If positioned in front, the coach should use a catch net as a shield. The batter hits five sets of four quick tosses with 10 seconds of rest between sets. The tosses should be very quick, giving the batter just enough time to reset between each toss. So, the rhythm is toss 1-2-3-4, rest 10 seconds, toss 1-2-3-4, and so on until all five sets are complete. The coach should toss each set to a different contact zone.

Coaching Points   Make sure the batter finishes the swing and resets to a balanced starting position. Some batters try to go too fast and shorten the follow-through, or they keep all of their weight on the front foot while executing the drill. In any drill, batters need to maintain proper swing fundamentals during the drill execution.

Variation   To make the drill more challenging, use weighted baseballs to provide more resistance so the bat speed must increase. You can purchase weighted baseballs, or you can make them yourself. Just get some old baseballs from a baseball coach and soak them in a bucket of water for two days. Leave them in the sun to dry for a couple of days, and you have weighted baseballs.

PITCH RECOGNITION

Purpose   This drill is great for helping batters to see the ball better and to learn to focus on the release point and match their motion with the pitcher. The drill is performed during pitching practices, and as a result, it helps the pitchers by giving them a live batter in the box to pitch to.

Execution   Wearing a protective helmet, the batter takes up her stance in the box. When the pitcher releases the pitch, the batter does everything physically and mentally to prepare to swing without actually hitting the ball. The batter calls out the pitch as soon as she recognizes it. In the beginning, batters will be way behind the pitchers and will not identify the pitch until it is in the catcher's glove. After many repetitions of this drill, batters will be able to not only identify the pitch early but also see the spins.

Coaching Points   This drill can also be used to help batters learn to adjust to the pitcher. Hitting is definitely a game of adjustment for both the batter and the pitcher. If the pitcher is slow and low, the batter must move up in the box. If the pitcher throws most pitches away, the batter should crowd. When the pitches are hard and lack movement, the batter should move to the back of the box in order to see the ball longer.

OVERHEAD TOSS

Purpose This is another good drill for helping batters learn to keep their eyes active and focused. In addition to working on focus, players will also be working to shorten their swing and minimize the movement in their swing. Major-league all-star Joe Mauer has stated on many occasions that this drill was one of the staples of his training regimen as a youth.

Execution The batter stands in the box. The coach uses a ball drop device (see figure 4.4) or the coach can stand on a lift, ladder, or scaffold and drop the ball into the contact zone from above. The batter must visually pick up the ball as it enters the contact zone and must execute proper swing fundamentals. The batter completes three sets of 10 repetitions.

Coaching Points Many commercial training aid companies have developed products such as overhead rollers or gravity drops that make this drill easier to set up.

Figure 4.4 Ball drop from above.

BALANCE

All great hitters say that balance is extremely important in their success. They talk about balance in the stance, stride, and swing. Balance is especially important to singles hitters and contact hitters who must trust their hands, avoid being anxious, and let the ball come into the zone. If the batter is off balance during any part of the swing, she will not have the bat control needed to hit the ball where she wants to hit it. A well-balanced batting stance gives the batter a solid attack foundation. Balance allows the batter to be relaxed and feel confident in her ability to hit any pitch. Proper balance keeps the head still and allows the batter to see the ball more clearly.

Balance is also important in bunting, and any player who strives for a high batting average must be a very good bunter. She must be proficient at bunting for a hit as well as a sacrifice bunt. When bunting, the batter needs to be balanced on the balls of the feet and must not lean forward or backward.

BALANCE BEAM

Purpose   Consistent work on the balance beam reinforces muscle memory and helps the player through all phases of the hitting cycle. This drill is a must-have station for every hitting circuit workout.

Execution   This drill requires a balance beam (see figure 4.5). The beam is a piece of 2-by-10-inch wood that is cut 4 feet long. The beam needs three support pieces made of 1-foot-long pieces of a 4-by-4-inch post. A support should be placed at each end of the beam, and one should be placed in the middle. Cover the top of the beam with Astroturf or a similar nonslip surface. The batter takes her normal batting position on the beam and takes full swings off of front tosses. The batter completes three sets of 10 repetitions.

Figure 4.5   (a) Batter on the beam and (b) the follow through.

Coaching Points   The best setup is to have two balance beams in a cage, one for right-handed batters and one for left-handed batters. This way you do not have to move the beam back and forth.

Variation   A second use for the balance beam is to help batters learn to avoid overstriding. To reinforce a short compact stride, have the batters set up 1 to 2 inches (2.5 to 5.0 cm) from the end of the board. From this position, if the batter overstrides, she will get feedback really quickly. One college coach we know takes his hitters to the pool, sets them up 1 to 2 inches from the end of the high-dive board, and has them execute dry swings. He swears they are balanced and do not overstride. Although it may work, we do not recommend this approach.

BOUNCING TENNIS BALLS

Purpose   In this drill, the batter works on loading and then striding to attack position. The drill enables the batter to work on the timing of these parts of the swing in relation to the ball.

Execution   To begin the drill, the coach takes a position in front and 45 degrees to the right of a right-handed batter (opposite for left-handed batters). Standing at an angle from the batter enables the coach to clearly observe the batter's entire lower body during the hitting process. The coach bounces tennis balls into the correct hitting zone. Bouncing tennis balls are more realistic than tosses because they require the batter to load on the bounce and time her stride to hit the ball as it reaches the optimum contact zone. The batter performs three sets of 10 repetitions.

Coaching Points   Balance is important to the loading, striding, and hitting that the batter does in this drill. If the batter is not balanced throughout, this will show immediately, and positive changes can be made. Coaches will quickly see problems such as overstriding, striding open, rolling the front foot, or landing on the front heel. All of these problems seriously affect the batter's balance and ability to hit for average. The drill also allows the coach to observe the load (or negative) move and to help the batter improve this portion of the swing. Another great benefit of this drill is the immediate feedback. The drill allows the coach to bounce the ball on any plane desired. For instance, if a batter is struggling with pitches that are low and in, the coach can bounce it there. If the batter's problems are up and away, the coach can bounce it there.

Variation   A variation of this drill is the standing toss. From the same position, the coach can toss to the batter at belt level and also observe every action within the hitting cycle. A good strategy is to begin with 20 bouncing tennis balls, which allows the coach to focus on the lower body and provide constructive feedback after each swing. Then switch to the upper-body toss with the same tennis balls from the same 45-degree angle. This enables the coach to observe the entire swing and help the batter make any necessary changes to the upper body.

HITTING TO ALL FIELDS

As mentioned earlier, high-average hitters must be able to hit the ball to all fields. This may be the most important skill for players who are not a home-run threat, who want to be major contributors, and who want to have a great batting average and on-base percentage. Several key mental and physical processes that are important to this skill have already been discussed: seeing the ball, knowing and recognizing pitches, and being balanced throughout the swing.

Now let's take a look at drills that players can do to increase their ability to hit to all fields. The important thing to remember in these drills (and when working to perfect any skill) is that repetition is critical. Three things will make players successful in any skill they attempt to perfect: confidence, discipline, and repetition. They must be confident that they can perform the skill; they must be disciplined so they do it right; and they must do it over and over. As noted previously, practice does not make perfect; perfect practice makes perfect.

The best hitters hit five days a week or more. They have the ability to hit up the middle, hit behind the runner, and pull the ball. These skills are honed through constant practice, and the drills in this section can help players learn them. When learning to hit to all fields, the batters first need to understand the three contact points. To pull the ball, they need to catch it a little in front of the plate. To hit the ball up the middle, they need to hit the ball in the contact zone. To hit the ball to the opposite field, they need to trust their hands and let the pitch in a little. Figure 4.6 illustrates the three hitting zones for a right-handed batter.

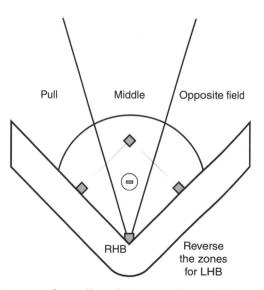

Figure 4.6   The hitting zones for pulling, hitting up the middle, and hitting to the opposite field.

Hitting the Ball up the Middle

Some hitters think that this is an easy skill to perfect. Hitting up the middle is definitely less challenging than hitting to the opposite field, but it still requires hard work and lots of repetitions. Nothing is easy when it comes to hitting that moving ball at high speed. The drills listed here will help batters learn to hit the ball up the middle.

TEE WITH STRING OR TEE TO TARGET

Purpose   This drill gives the batter a visual aid for hitting the ball up the middle and provides instant feedback about the hits.

Execution   This drill should be performed in front of a net or in a batting cage. Set up a tee with a string by attaching one end of an 8-foot (2.4 m) string to the stem of the tee and attaching the other end to a net or to the cage directly in line with where the pitcher would be in a game (figure 4.7). The batter practices hitting off the tee and attempts to stay long through the ball and drive the ball into the net on a parallel path with the string. The batter performs three sets of 10 repetitions.

Figure 4.7   Tee with string setup.

Coaching Points   The batter's goal is for the ball to travel along the path of the string, moving directly back toward where a pitcher and center fielder would be positioned. Another cue for the batter is to try to keep her barrel on the plane with the string for as long as possible.

Variation   A variation of this drill is to place the tee about 8 feet in front of a target square placed on the side of the cage or net; the target square can be made with athletic tape. The batter then tries to consistently hit the ball from the tee into the target.

FRONT TOSS OR LIVE PITCHING INTO A NET

Purpose   In this drill, batters learn the correct contact point for hitting up the middle, and they receive immediate feedback. The batters also learn to stay long through the ball. In addition, the batters develop muscle memory, which helps them succeed in future at-bats.

Execution   The coach or a hitting partner stands behind a pitching screen that is approximately 15 to 20 feet (4.5 to 6.1 m) from the batter. Another screen behind the pitcher has a target or gap in the middle that is slightly to the left of the pitcher (see figure 4.8). The batter tries to hit as many balls as she can into the screen and specifically into the target or gap. Great players are very competitive, so this drill can be made into a competition: Give the batter 10 points for hitting the target and 5 points for hitting the net. Take away points if the batter misses the net altogether. The batter completes three sets of 10 thrown balls.

Figure 4.8   Batting into the screen target.

Coaching Points   Players need to keep the bat in a long hitting zone through the swing and follow through.

TRIPLE TEE

Purpose   This drill helps batters learn how to stay long through the ball and how to drive the ball up the middle.

Execution   Set up a standard double or triple tee (one that has two or three stem holes) so that the back stem is at the contact point for hitting up the middle, the next one or two stems are lined up in a row in front of the back stem, and all the stems are about 6 inches (15.2 cm) apart (see figure 4.9). Place one ball on the top of each of the stems. The batter makes contact with the back ball and

Figure 4.9   Batting with a triple tee.

tries to hit that ball directly into the ball in front, which then knocks off the third ball. If the batter hits the first ball square and stays long through it, she will have a good chance of making the next two balls travel up the middle as well. The next two balls provide a visual aid for keeping the barrel in the zone a long time.

Coaching Points   This is a simple but effective drill. The batter must work hard and concentrate on driving each ball into the front ball. In this drill, a helpful tactic for the batter is to pretend that she is trying to make contact with all three balls; this will help her stay long through the ball that she is actually hitting.

Pulling the Ball

Many people think that pulling the ball is the easiest zone for hitters. Most ballparks, from major league to youth league, have shorter fences down the lines. And most young players start out as pull hitters. Many hitters are classified as pull hitters because they do not have the ability to keep their weight centered, and therefore they get out on their front foot ahead of the pitch. These hitters are usually anxious in the box. They do not trust their hands, and because of that, they are way ahead of the pitch. In many instances, anxious batters foul off a couple of inside pitches and then strike out on a ball away or a changeup. These are hitters who hit .600 from the foul line to the dugout, but they usually don't hit for a high average.

Pulling the ball should be a choice, not a constant. High-average hitters have the ability to hit to all fields. Each situation and pitch dictates where they will hit the ball. With reaction time being so fast in softball, batters should not step differently when attempting to pull the ball. One cardinal rule is to never try to pull an outside pitch.

The best way to work on pulling the ball is to practice hitting off a standard tee or front toss. Remember, a batter should not open up for an inside pitch unless that is her normal stance. If a batter is being jammed, she can get farther away from the plate. However, she should also remember that getting farther off the plate gives her less coverage on the outside pitch. Players should work on pulling the ball as part of their daily tee work. In fact, hitters should hit balls to their pull field, up the middle, and to the opposite field each day. Developing the ability to be a good pull hitter is easier than hitting to the opposite field, but it still requires practice.

TENNESSEE ZONES

Purpose   Using target zones gives the batter a visual aid and immediate feedback on her ability to hit to all areas of the field.

Execution   Use cones to divide the field into three separate hitting zones (see figure 4.10). A batter starts in the batter's box. The coach provides front tosses to the batter. The coach calls out a zone before the pitch, and the batter attempts to drive the ball to that zone. By using front toss, the coach can try to put the pitch where it is easier for the batter to succeed. For instance, the coach should not call "Zone 1" to a right-handed batter and then throw the pitch outside. Players love to compete, so points can be awarded for hitting to the correct zone (and points can be taken away for missing the designated zone). The batter completes 10 swings, and then the rest of the batters in the lineup can move through the drill.

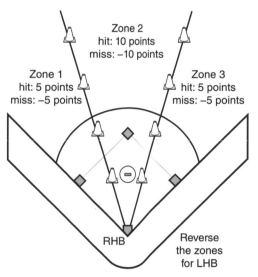

Figure 4.10   Cone setup and zones.

Coaching Points   When a player is struggling to perform a particular skill, such as hitting to a zone, coaches tend to focus on correcting body mechanics. However, often the most helpful thing that a coach can do is establish a visual target for the batter. When a visual target is included in the drill, a player's body has a way of making a physical adjustment in order to achieve the desired result.

Variation   This drill can also be performed using a pitching machine or a live pitcher. Initially, either of these options will be much more difficult for the batter.

Hitting to the Opposite Field

As most softball books and hitting coaches will confirm, hitting the ball to the opposite field is the toughest hitting skill to learn. The high-average hitter develops this skill through hundreds of hours of practice. Also referred to as hitting behind the runner, this is a highly valued skill because it can be used as part of a team strategy in the hit-and-run or in just trying to advance the runner. How many times have you seen a right-handed batter hit the ball to the left side of the field with runners on first and second base? The defense gets an easy force at third and often a double play. The player with the ability to hit to all fields—and especially to hit behind the runner—is worth her weight in gold.

Two things are essential to this skill. First, the batter needs to use an inside-out swing where the hands lead the bat head to the ball. The hands should stay a little closer to the body as they move to the ball. If the hands extend too early, the batter will have a tougher time hitting the outside pitch. Second, the batter must trust her hands and allow the ball to get farther into the hitting zone. Several drills can be used to help hitters become more proficient in hitting the ball to the opposite field. The drills in this section are helpful for learning this skill. The Tennessee Zones drill presented in the previous section is also a great drill for this purpose (the coach should stress hitting behind the runner).

TEE DRILL FOR OPPOSITE FIELD

Purpose This drill helps batters learn the basic fundamentals of hitting to the opposite field.

Execution Set up a tee on the outside of the plate and even with the batter's belly button to simulate letting the ball farther into the hitting zone. The batter takes up her normal batting position and works on hitting the ball to the opposite field (right field for a right-handed batter; left field for a left-handed batter). The batter takes 10 swings, and then the rest of the batters in the lineup rotate through. When performing this drill in a cage, the batter must understand where her target area is located to simulate a successful hit to the opposite field.

Coaching Points The batter's hands must stay close to the body and lead the bat head. If the barrel extends too early and gets even with or ahead of the hands, the batter will know this immediately because the ball will travel up the middle or to the pull field. Make sure the batter doesn't start stepping toward the tee. Instead, she should maintain the same stride that she would in a live game situation—directly toward the pitcher.

FRONT TOSS FROM CLOSE RANGE

Purpose   This drill is similar to the previous drill, except a moving ball is added to the drill, which provides a bigger challenge as the batter continues to work on the fundamentals of hitting to the opposite field.

Execution   The batter takes up her normal position at the plate. The coach tosses the ball to the outside corner of the plate, working on pitches low and away as well as pitches up and away. The batter needs to trust her hands, let the ball in, and hit the ball to the opposite field. If in the cage, the batter must hit the ball to the opposite side of the cage. The batter completes two sets of 10 repetitions.

Coaching Points   When batters know that they are working on opposite-field hitting and that the toss or pitch is being thrown outside, they have a tendency to anticipate and stride in that direction. Batters must step directly toward the pitcher, just like in a live game situation. In a live situation, the batter strides before knowing the pitch location.

NO POP, NO PULL

Purpose   This drill teaches batters to use the inside-out swing, and it is a more advanced drill than the previous two drills. In this drill, the batter learns to let the ball in, stay level, and drive the ball to the opposite field on a line.

Execution   The coach or partner feeds balls to the batter using front toss or a machine; live pitching can also be used in this drill. The person feeding the balls to the batter works the outside of the plate. The batter receives a set of 15 pitches and uses the inside-out swing to hit the balls. The goal is to hit the ball on a line (no pop) and to the opposite field (no pull). The batter is also assigned a total of 15 sprints from home to first that she will complete after the hitting set. However, for every properly executed swing, the sprint count is reduced by one. This normally results in immediate improvement after a few days. Another positive thing about this drill is that while the players are learning, they are also conditioning.

Coaching Points   For batters who are just starting to work on the inside-out swing, one common problem is dipping the shoulder and popping the ball up in the air. In this drill, the batter receives immediate visual feedback if she drops the shoulder and pops the ball up.

DOUBLE TEE

Purpose This drill reinforces the difference in the contact zone for inside and outside pitches.

Execution Use a double tee and place two stems to simulate hitting the inside pitch and hitting the outside pitch (figure 4.11). The batter first hits the inside pitch, trying to hit a fair ball to left field, preferably a line drive. Then the batter hits the outside pitch, working to hit a line drive to right field. The placement of the tee stems helps the batter learn to make contact farther in front for the inside pitch and deeper in the zone for the outside pitch. After the second hit, the player can set up again and repeat the drill for the desired number of repetitions.

Figure 4.11 Batting from the *(a)* inside and *(b)* outside tees.

Coaching Points Make sure the batter is striding directly toward the pitcher for both the inside pitch and the outside pitch. Players often get lazy with this, especially when working off a tee. The batter needs to set up in a place where she can be balanced all through the swing on both contact points.

The only way to become consistent in this skill is to practice, practice, and practice some more. When the batter becomes proficient off the tee and in the cages, she should hit on the field and try to put the ball exactly where she wants it to go. Batters with high batting averages are confident in their ability to execute under pressure. Players can only execute under pressure if they have done it so many times in practice that it is just second nature. Be sure to work inside, middle, and outside. When we worked with hitters on the U.S.

Olympic teams in 1996 and 2000, one thing stood out very clearly: All of the top hitters had the ability to hit to all fields. One player we worked with—who was a top hitter worldwide—began practice every day off a tee; she would hit 25 balls to the pull field, 25 up the middle, and 25 to the opposite field.

ADJUSTING TO THE PITCHER

As mentioned earlier, high-average hitters study the pitcher from the dugout and learn what pitches she throws. They also play the game one pitch at a time and learn from each at-bat. Batters should not be "guess hitters." They should have a plan for what pitch they are looking to hit each at-bat and be prepared to attack that pitch when it comes. With two strikes batters maintain an aggressive approach but must expand the hitting zone to the entire strike zone. The best hitters think about possible adjustments in the dugout and in the on-deck circle, and they are also able to make adjustments in the batter's box.

Most adjustments made in the batter's box are simple and come easy to experienced hitters. Amazingly, many hitters never adjust during an at-bat or even during an entire game. Some hitters strike out again and again when a pitcher is throwing them low and away. The amazing thing is that those hitters remain in the back of the box and neither they nor their coaches make any adjustments.

Here are some common adjustments that batters can make in the box:

- If the batter is being jammed constantly, she should get off the plate a little more.
- If the pitcher is pitching away from the batter, the batter should crowd the plate.
- If the pitcher is slow and low, the batter should get way up in the box and catch the pitch before it drops.
- If the pitcher is throwing hard with little movement, the batter should get as far back in the box as she can.
- If the ball is breaking up just before it gets to the batter, she should move up and try to get it before the break.

A good time to work on these adjustments is in practice. The best drill for this is the Pitch Recognition drill described on page 75. Good hitters like to stand in when pitchers are throwing in practice because it helps them learn how to see the ball and how to make adjustments. Standing in the batter's box during live pitching drills also helps the batter gauge speeds and see various spins. Pitchers also like this because they get better when working with a live batter in the box. This is called a double-win drill.

As mentioned, a player should have a mental game plan. In addition, the player needs to develop a hitting plan for each game. A player's hitting plan should list her goals during four phases of the game: in pregame batting practice, in the dugout, in the on-deck circle, and in the batter's box. This hitting plan should combine the player's desired mental and physical response during each of the four phases.

With the tools provided in this chapter, a player can become a high-average hitter. Success in any endeavor starts with desire and motivation, and skills are perfected through dedication to excellence. Success is in the mind's eye, and if a player believes she can do something, she will. Perfection is difficult to achieve, but if a player strives for perfection, she will definitely achieve excellence.

CHAPTER 5

Hitting for Power

Chapter 4 covered hitting for average, including the characteristics of high-average hitters along with drills to help players improve their batting average and on-base percentage. In this chapter, we discuss power hitting. Everyone knows the great impact that power hitting has on the game. Power hitters are a special breed, and the physical and mental skills that most power hitters possess are somewhat different from those of the high-average hitters. Power hitters sell tickets and draw crowds at every level of the game because everyone loves the home run or the double in the gap. Most power hitters do not hit for a high average. In college softball leagues (as in major-league baseball), the power hitter is more of a risk taker. Power hitters swing from the heels and go for the fence. They strike out a lot. Their main statistics are runs batted in and slugging percentage.

Ideally, a team will include a combination of all the types of hitters described in this book. A championship team has a place for everyone. If a team is versatile, the team will usually have a very good winning percentage. Our offensive strategy is to have players who hit for a high average in the 1, 2, and 9 slots. The 9th batter is considered a second leadoff batter. These three batters are typically slappers who can also hit away and have a high average. Batter 3 has the best combination of power and high average and the versatility to play small ball (bunt and steal) when necessary. Batters 4, 5, 6, and 7 are the power hitters who drive in most of the runs. The 8th batter is a high-average hitter who can also run a little and can hit the ball into the gap.

CHARACTERISTICS OF POWER HITTERS

Three characteristics are most commonly associated with power hitting. First, power hitters are free swingers. Second, power hitters use a slight uppercut in their swing. Third, power hitters contact the ball in front of the plate. Power hitters also usually possess the following characteristics:

- Good eyesight
- Strong wrists
- Strength
- Very good bat speed
- Great hip rotation
- Powerful weight shift
- Extension and finishing high

Mentally, power hitters cannot be afraid to fail. They must understand that as free swingers or go-for-broke hitters, they will strike out more than the contact or high-average hitters. They normally do not possess the same skills as those players who hit for a high average. Baserunning, hitting to all fields, and a good short game are not part of their repertoire. They hit the ball hard, hit it where it is pitched, and try to hit it deep every time. One short-game skill that will help the power hitter (and her team) is the ability to bunt. Most opposing coaches will have their defensive corners playing back when the power hitter is at the plate with a fast base runner on third. We have scored a lot of runs over the years by having the power hitter execute the squeeze bunt. This is a high-percentage play when the corners are back.

A player does not have to be big to be a power hitter. Many average-size players can hit for power. As mentioned, this skill requires strong wrists, strength, and good bat speed, but technique and fundamentals are more important than size. We have a player who is five-foot-four and wiry, but she possesses all the required traits. She has strong rhythm and movement before the swing, and she attacks the ball with her whole body. This player does not look like the prototype long-ball hitter, but last year she hit home runs to beat two top-ranked teams. When she does not hit the ball out, she can drive it in the gap and to the wall. Do not confuse size with power. Power hitters come in all sizes. As the saying goes, "it is not the size of the dog in the fight, it is the size of the fight in the dog."

KEY SWING MECHANICS FOR POWER HITTING

For a player to develop into a power hitter, certain swing mechanics are essential. The player must understand the role that her hips, hands, and legs play in creating a powerful swing.

Role of the Hips

When a batter is hitting for power, the hips must lead the hands. To be effective hitting the long ball, the batter needs to use a slight uppercut swing. If the batter can get the ball into the air, it has a good chance of going out. Most power hitters cock their hips (see figure 5.1) and strive for loft on the ball. If the batter swings up, even slightly, she needs to lead with the hips and finish high. We always tell our hitters to attack on contact and to make believe that two other balls are out there to hit as they finish the swing. Players who do not use their hips are generally ineffective and become an arm or wrist hitter. The hips give a batter the ability to get the entire body

Figure 5.1 Cocking the hips.

into the swing. Watch the great golfers. They really use the hips to lead the hands. Like softball players, golfers need the long ball, and the full-body swing is the only way to get it consistently.

Hands

The batter always wants to be palm up, palm down at contact (see figure 5.2). The power hand is the top hand; the directional hand is the bottom hand. The directional hand will lead the slight loft or uppercut. People have varying opinions on when the batter should take the top hand off the bat during the power swing. Most batters find it easier and less restrictive to release the top hand near the end of the finish (see figure 5.3). This allows the batter to finish high with full power and not be restricted in any way near the end of the swing.

Figure 5.2 Palm up and palm down hand position.

Stride

For power hitting, the prestride stance for most women is different from the stance used by male hitters because women generally do not possess the upper-body strength that men have. Women with that kind of strength are few and far between. In nine years with the U.S. Olympic team, I saw only two female

Figure 5.3 Top hand releases at finish.

hitters who had upper-body strength comparable with men. They were two of the strongest female players in the world. Women can still be tremendous power hitters, however. The key is using the legs and hips to provide maximum power, rather than relying on upper-body strength alone.

For women to use the hips effectively in the power swing, the stride needs to be short and compact. The power hitter must not have a real wide stance. She should start with her feet just outside the shoulders (see figure 5.4). This allows her to get her hips into the ball with more authority. To simulate this, stand with your hands on your hips. Take up an extra wide stance. Stride and

Figure 5.4 Proper stance for power hitting.

Figure 5.5 The power stride.

open your hips. You will quickly see that you cannot get the needed hip thrust with the wide stance. Now stand with your feet just outside the shoulders. Stride and open your hips. You will get the thrust that you need.

The power stride is aggressive, balanced, and closed (see figure 5.5). The stride is generally no more than a few inches; a stride that is too long can cause the batter to lose balance and leg drive. The batter should step directly toward the pitcher. The batter must maintain good balance during her stride, keeping her weight inside her knees, so that she is able to generate good leg drive through contact.

PITCH SELECTION

Pitch selection is a difficult challenge for hitters in every offensive strategy. Power hitters are by nature "free swingers." They think, *See the ball, hit the ball.* A pitcher with any knowledge of pitching strategy or specific knowledge of the hitter is not going to groove it when the batter comes to the plate. The pitcher's job is to neutralize the batter and to get the batter to swing at a low-percentage pitch. When have you seen a pitcher groove the first pitch to a batter in a bunting situation? When have you seen a pitcher throw the batter a pitch up in the zone when a runner is on third with less than two outs? These things do not happen. In the bunt situation, the pitcher will most likely throw a rise ball in an attempt to get the batter to pop up the bunt and double the runner. In a sacrifice fly situation, the pitcher will likely throw a pitch down and away in an attempt to induce a ground ball.

The battle between the pitcher and the batter is the essence of the game. We often tell our hitters the following: "Either you control the plate, or the pitcher controls the plate." There is no in-between. The best strategy for the batter is to know what her pitch is and know exactly where she wants it. The batter should look for her pitch and should not swing at anything else (unless she has two strikes and needs to foul the pitch off). Yes, power hitters are free swingers, and that can play right into the pitcher's hand. A power hitter should strive to be different. She wants to be a power hitter who is always dangerous but also selective. Remember, a pitch that is up in the zone is always easier to hit out than a drop that is down and out of the zone.

Figure 5.6 is a chart that a batter can use to identify her zone and her pitch. The batter should number the hitting zones from 1 to 9, with 1 being her favorite pitch zone and 9 being her least favorite. This chart gives the coach and the hitter information regarding what pitches the hitter likes to hit best and least. Using this information, the coach can remind the hitter what pitches to look for when she is in favorable counts (0-0, 1-0, 2-0, 3-0, 2-1,

High out	High middle	High in
Middle out	Middle	Middle in
Low out	Low middle	Low in

Figure 5.6 Hitting zone chart for a right-handed batter. The chart is from the pitcher's perspective. For a left-handed batter, switch the in and out columns.

3-1) and wants to swing at only her best pitches. Knowing what pitches the hitter is least confident against is also helpful and allows the hitter to work on her weaknesses. A batter should use this information and should be selective. She should get her pitch!

DEVELOPING LONG-BALL SKILLS

Hitting the long ball or becoming a "gapper rapper" is a skill that takes hours and hours of practice. As mentioned earlier, mastering any skill requires confidence, discipline, and repetition. So how does a hitter become a deep threat? How does she gain that confidence and discipline? The simple answer is through repetition. The hitter must start by achieving a certain degree of strength. Then she must develop a hitting plan. The plan needs to specify the hitter's goals as well as the time lines for achieving those goals. The plan should identify the drills and the number of repetitions the player will complete each day. The plan should also contain a method for measuring improvement. The old adage "a person who fails to plan plans to fail" applies to the skill of hitting.

Figure 5.7 provides a sample form that may be used to create a hitting plan. The form is designed so that it can be used by every hitter and for every phase of the hitting cycle. Once the player has determined her goals, she should make

Figure 5.7   Sample Hitting Plan

Player: _____ Date: _____

Specific goal: _____ *[The goal should specify exactly what the player wants to achieve with the plan.]* _____
_____
_____

Beginning date: _____*[Date the player expects to start working toward the goal]* _____

Target date: _____ *[Date the player believes she will master the skill]* _____

Specific drills to be used: _____ *[Drills that the player will use to improve in the skill area targeted]* _____
_____

Frequency of practice: _____ *[Number of times per week or month that the player will work on the skill]*
_____
_____

Number of repetitions for each drill: _____ *[Example: High Tee, 3 sets of 10; Tee With String, 3 sets of 10]* _____
_____

Method of measuring progress: _____ *[Example: For bat speed, measure speed every 2 weeks]* ____
_____
_____

Player's signature of completion: _____

a plan that is designed to help her achieve those goals. Remember, goals must be specific, realistic, and attainable. A critical part of the plan is the method of measuring progress. The method will vary depending on the skill that the player is trying to improve. In some cases, specific measurements will need to be taken at specific intervals. In other cases, the coach may simply evaluate the player's progress by observing the player perform the skill.

When possible, hitters should also consult a personal trainer. High school and college players may have access to a strength and conditioning expert. As stated previously, power hitters will need a certain degree of strength to hit the long ball. The hitter also needs quick hands and powerful wrists. Long-ball hitters usually have a strong lower body and powerful hips. Although much of an athlete's strength is genetic, a strength and conditioning expert can suggest drills and exercises to help the player develop stronger legs, hips, core muscles, arms, and wrists—all areas that are key to power hitting. If a player doesn't have access to an expert in this area, other resources such as videos and books are available for general strength training. *Sports Power* by David Sandler (Champaign, IL: Human Kinetics, 2005) is an excellent starting point.

Once a player has a plan in place and has set her goals, it's time for her to work on her fundamentals. Hitting for power requires a lot of work. Here's something you will often hear people say about the practice habits of an All-American or other outstanding athlete: "She was the first to arrive and the last to leave." One of the best ways for players to work on their fundamentals is to perform dry swings in front of a mirror. The following drill can help players do just that.

1-2-3 DRILL

Purpose   This drill, also known as shadow swings, provides continuous reinforcement of the correct fundamentals that are essential to the success of the long-ball hitter. This is a great drill to perform inside because it does not require the player to hit a ball.

Execution   The player takes up her stance and faces a mirror about 10 feet (3 m) directly in front of her. The mirror should be at the same angle that the pitcher would be at. For maximum effectiveness, players should do 25 repetitions of this drill each day. Players complete the drill in three phases:

1. The player checks her stance, balance, hand positions, knee flex, and head angle in the mirror; then she says "one." On this count, the player executes her load or negative move, watching her movement in the mirror the whole time. After checking that her fundamentals are okay, the player then says "two."

2. On the count of two, the player strides and puts herself in position to attack the pitch. At this stage of the hitting cycle, the player must make certain that when she achieves the toe touch, her weight remains balanced, and her hands are cocked to begin the swing. The player should check these items in the mirror. When these items are correct, the player says "three."

3. On the count of three, the player executes the swing. She plants her front heel and drives her legs while swinging the bat. The key points here are that the hips lead the hands; the hands are palm up, palm down at contact; and the swing has a high finish. The long-ball hitter will need a slight loft in her swing. The batter must attack on contact and continue to attack until the bat finishes against her back.

Coaching Points   After the one count, the player should look for correct foot width, proper bending at the waist and knees, correct bat angle, and proper hand position in relation to the body. On the two count, getting into the attack position is especially important for long-ball hitters because so much of their success is based on balance and timing. The player should make sure that the stride is short and compact, directly toward the pitcher, and most important, closed or only slightly open to the pitcher. In the third phase, a common mistake for young hitters is cutting the finish short and letting the bat stop at the front arm instead of ending lightly against the back. Cutting the follow-through short will decrease the distance potential, the bat speed, and the power of the swing.

Variation   A coach can use this drill when working one on one with players; in this case, a mirror is not needed. When the coach is present, he or she can make immediate changes or recommendations throughout the hitting cycle. The coach can also provide positive feedback when the player has worked hard and developed strong fundamentals.

Many of the drills explained in chapter 4 are also used by long-ball hitters and should be incorporated into their hitting plan. All of the bat speed drills in chapter 6—including the Throwing Bats drill and the Quick Toss With Weighted Balls drill—are very important for the power hitter. The drill that involves using a weighted bat and large weighted balls is particularly useful for these hitters. Power hitters will also benefit from resistance training of any type.

Several other drills are designed specifically for the long-ball or power hitter. Each of these drills will help power hitters become more efficient and productive. In some of the drills, the hitter can actually see success and watch the ball being hit or going over the fence. There is no substitution for the confidence gained when a hitter sees that she can consistently hit the long ball. Let's look at a few of these drills, starting with the most basic.

HIP ROTATION DRILL

Purpose   In this lower-body drill, the batter learns to lead with the hips and thrust with the hips.

Execution   The tee is positioned directly even with the batter's belly button. The batter places the bat behind her back and at the top of her hips. If she is a right-handed batter, the barrel is pointed to her right (opposite for a left-handed batter). She holds the bat against her backside using both arms and balancing the bat lightly against the inside of her wrists (see figure 5.8). The batter cocks her hips, loads, and then strides. The batter then leads with the hips, rotates, and strikes the ball with the barrel of the bat. With the bat held behind her back, the batter must completely rotate the hips to strike the ball. She should complete 10 to 15 repetitions.

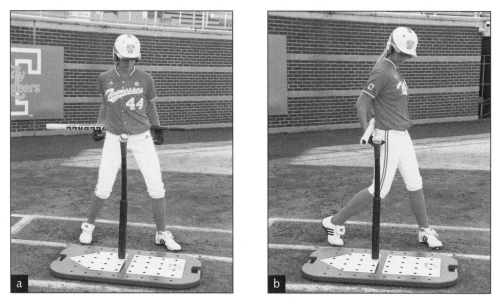

Figure 5.8   *(a)* Position for holding the bat and *(b)* contact position.

Coaching Points   This drill is elementary but is very important for young hitters. Coaches should include this drill in every basic hitting circuit and in every instructional camp. This drill can also be helpful for older, more experienced hitters who are struggling with lower-body rotation.

Variation   For younger players, a dowel can be used instead of a bat. The dowel, which can be purchased at any hardware store, should be about 2 to 3 inches (5.1 to 7.6 cm) in diameter and 34 to 36 inches (86.4 to 91.4 cm) in length.

HIGH TEE ON HOME PLATE

Purpose   This drill enables the batter to practice keeping her hands high and above the ball, swinging through the ball (getting great extension and a long finish), and driving the ball over the fence if possible.

Execution   The batter starts at home plate with a high tee (chest high). The batter has a bucket of balls to feed the tee, or a coach may serve as the feeder. The batter takes 30 cuts, trying to hit the ball out of the park on every cut (figure 5.9). The batter is working on correct fundamentals, bat speed, loft, and finishing long through the ball. Batters should hit the first 10 up the middle, adjust the position of the tee, hit the second 10 to left field, then adjust the tee again and hit the last 10 to right field. Coaches may want to chart where each of the 30 hits goes and allow the batter to review her progress from day to day.

Figure 5.9   *(a)* Hitting off a high tee and *(b)* the follow through.

Coaching Points   Two things to stress in this drill are the plane of the swing and the finish. A coach can also stress that the batters need to hit to all fields and go with the pitch in order to be successful. When a hitter—either a power hitter or high-average hitter—cannot hit to all fields, she is much easier to defend. This is often seen during major-league baseball games when defenses shift for certain hitters and invite them to hit into an unguarded area. Practice and encouragement will help batters hit to all fields. Coaches should stay on them and stress the importance of being a hitter who is difficult to defend. All these skills can be enhanced through this simple tee drill.

(continued)

High Tee on Home Plate (continued)

Variation This drill can be used to play a modified form of home-run derby. Two or three hitters compete to hit the most home runs. The players are given 1 point for a ball that hits the fence on one bounce, 2 points for a ball that hits the fence in the air, and 3 points for a home run. This game really gets the blood flowing and inserts a little pressure on the players. It helps the coach identify which players are good competitors and which players struggle when faced with a challenge.

MACHINE AND CAGE DRILL

Purpose This drill gives the batter a visual cue and target for hitting the long ball when doing her hitting workout in a cage.

Execution The drill works well when done in a 65-foot (19.8 m) batting cage with a 20-foot (6.1 m) ceiling. Use a pitching machine that is set to throw pitches at waist to chest height, or the top part of the strike zone. The pitching machine should be set at 63 to 65 miles per hour. The feeder stands behind a protective screen and simulates the pitching motion, finishing at the simulated release point (approximately where a live pitcher would release the ball). The batter should match motion with the simulation—loading, striding, and then contacting the ball about 1.5 feet (0.5 m) in front of the plate. The batter should work to establish a slight loft in the swing. She should try to drive the ball on a line up the middle so that it hits the very top middle of the cage, over 60 feet (18.3 m) from the point of impact. The ball should be a line drive, not a pop-up, which would hit the top of the cage early in its path. The batter should not pull the ball either, which would result in the ball striking the side of the cage early in its path. The batter should hit one set of 25 balls.

Coaching Points A striking difference between the power hitter and the high-average hitter is that most hitters who hit for average are taught to swing level or even slightly down. Some coaches tell players that the swing should be like chopping down a tree. This might work for high-average hitters (although we advocate a level swing), but it will not work for power hitters. The key to initiating the slight uppercut is that the front hip must come around and come up slightly at contact.

Variation The drill can become a competition between players. Select a target zone where the back netting meets the top netting of the cage. This is the bull's-eye, or optimum spot to hit. Each player will get 20 swings. A player scores 2 points for hitting the bull's-eye area, 1 point for hitting the back net below that area on a line, and 0 points for hitting anywhere else in the cage (hitting the top net too close to the batter, hitting the side nets, or hitting the ground before striking the net). There is nothing like competition between players to increase the intensity level and focus.

FULL-FIELD POWER DRILL

Purpose This drill teaches hitters to hit the long ball. It also gives hitters instant visual feedback about their swings. There is no substitute for players seeing themselves performing a skill correctly. Hitters who drive ball after ball to and over the fence in practice will be comfortable hitting in a game. They know that they have the swing and power to hit the ball out because they have done it hundreds of times in practice. When hitters are able to relate the feel of the swing to the visual outcome, they can begin to make adjustments on their own.

Execution Use the newest (hardest) softballs you have on hand for this drill so that the batters have a better chance of hitting the ball over the fence. Set up three hitting stations as follows (see figure 5.10): a chest-high tee just outside the portable backstop, even with home plate, on the third-base side; a tee at home plate inside the portable backstop; and a chest-high tee, just outside the portable backstop, on the first-base side. Set a line of cones in left center field and right center field. The tee placements at the stations on either side of home plate will change for a left-handed batter (she will be pulling the ball

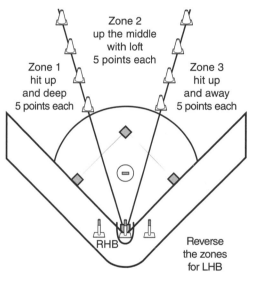

Figure 5.10 Setup for hitting stations.

to right field, so the tee will be out in front of the plate; she will also need the tee deeper in her hitting zone for the ball hit to left field).

Each player gets 15 swings at each of the three stations. On the third-base side, the batter tries to generate power from a stationary ball and drive the pitch both up and deep. This station requires the balls to be hit in zone 1. At home plate, the batter tries to hit the ball up the middle with loft, trying to keep the ball in zone 2. The batter on the first-base side is simulating letting the ball in, and she tries to drive the ball up and away to zone 3. Have a manager or assistant coach score each of the 45 swings. This person should score the accuracy, distance, and loft of each hit. The objectives for each tee and zone will be reversed for a left-handed batter.

Coaching Points When hitting for power, players must always remember two key points: extension and follow-through (or finish). Remember, the longer the barrel stays on the path of the ball, the better chance the batter has of being successful. Also, the batter must remember to make contact using

(continued)

Full-Field Power Drill *(continued)*

a slight uppercut swing and to stay on the ball as long as possible. When the batter makes contact, she should visualize other balls in the path, and she should strike these balls hard. Another benefit of this drill is that it provides defensive practice for the outfielders. If the batters execute well, the outfielders get deep fly balls, and they can work on crashing into the fence or fielding fly balls in the sun.

CHAPTER 6

Bat Speed

Studies completed by both Major League Baseball and the U.S. national team have shown that for every 10 miles per hour that a batter gains in bat speed, the batter picks up 30 to 40 feet in distance. Until very recently, the importance of bat speed was relatively unknown in most softball circles. This changed when several of the top hitting teams in Division 1 softball started measuring the bat speed of their players.

As coaches studied the effect of bat speed on their hitters, some important things became evident. They learned that bat speed is a measurement that changes not only with age but also with body size, athletic ability, and strength. They also learned that poor fundamentals, such as sweeping and casting, decrease a player's bat speed. Finally, coaches were able to establish norms for players from high school through the national or pro level.

TESTING BAT SPEED

Most college softball coaches have purchased bat speed meters (see figure 6.1) for use within their programs and in their summer camps. Good bat speed meters cost between $400 and $500 and are available through most sporting goods dealers or catalogues. The knowledge gained and the increased offensive output will make the bat speed meter a good purchase.

However, paying for a bat speed meter can be a challenge for youth, summer, and high school coaches. For teams at these levels, a good car wash or a booster club donation can make the purchase of a meter a little easier. In the interim, most college camps that teach hitting have bat speed meters, as do most hitting facilities. Players can get their bat speed measured at one of these camps or at a hitting facility.

At Tennessee, we have a bat speed program and a batting cage dedicated to bat speed drills. We call this cage Bat Speed Boulevard. We also measure the bat speed of our players once a month. We use the following norms to evaluate the bat speed of hitters in our programs and camps:

- Youth ball players (ages 12 to 15) = 40 to 50 mph
- High school players (ages 16 to 18) = 50 to 65 mph
- College players (ages 18 to 21) = 65 to 90 mph
- National team or professional league players = 75 to 95 mph

Some players exceed these norms, but most players do

Figure 6.1 Bat speed meter.

not have the bat speed they need to compete at their level of play. Only once in my nine years with the national team did I see a player exceed 100 mph when measured. That player hit cleanup for Team USA for years and is well known for her power and distance. Most of the select players on the U.S. team exceeded 80 mph. On the other hand, at Tennessee, we have seen incoming freshmen who were high school All-Americans come into our program with a bat speed of 40 to 45 mph.

Many players think they have the right bat speed but have never been tested. They don't have any idea what their actual bat speed is or how they can improve it. The first year that we started testing and improving bat speed at Tennessee, we led the nation in hitting. We think our players' batting averages increased because we emphasized bat speed in our hitting circuits and measured the players every two weeks. Some of our players increased their bat speed from 50 mph to 70 mph within a month.

An increase in bat speed allows a batter to trust her hands and let the ball in a little more before she commits. Coaches often talk about hitters who have "quick hands" and how important that is to successful hitting. Players with great bat speed are able to read the pitch longer before they make a decision to swing. Pitchers try to make their pitches move or break just before getting to the plate. A hitter with good bat speed will be able to read the break before committing to the swing. As a result, this hitter can avoid swinging at a pitch that is out of the zone, or she can adjust her barrel to where the ball is breaking in order to make better contact. The hitter with lesser bat speed has to make decisions earlier; because of this, she will likely swing at more pitches that eventually move out of the strike zone. Therefore, better bat speed will help improve pitch selection, which will lead to an increase in on-base percentage (because the hitter will draw more walks) and batting average (because the hitter will swing at better pitches).

An increase in bat speed also gives a hitter more power and distance. A bat traveling faster at the point of contact will result in the ball being driven farther when it is hit (force × speed = distance). In addition, when a hitter's quick hands allow her to see the ball longer before making a decision, she is able to make good decisions on pitch selection and thus swing at better pitches. It follows that when a hitter swings at better pitches, she is more likely to hit the ball square, which generally leads to the ball traveling a greater distance.

BAT SPEED DRILLS

The drills in this section have proven to increase players' bat speed. By using these drills, players develop stronger wrists and improve their fast-twitch muscles. Additionally, players enjoy these drills. When using drills that involve weighted bats or balls, the coach must be sure to stress fundamentals. Some players, especially younger players, will sacrifice fundamentals to complete the drill. This is counterproductive. Most of these drills can be used by players who are 12 or older, but the weights of the bats and balls must be appropriate for the age and size of the hitter. We use most of these drills in our camps, but again, we adjust them relative to the age and size of the campers.

In practice, hitters need to see fast pitches, either off a machine or from a live pitcher. Many players can be amazing hitters off the tee or off the front toss at 40 to 45 mph. The real challenge comes when the ball is pitched at top speed for the player's age level. When the pitches start coming in at top speed, a hitter's fundamentals often break down as she tries to speed up her swing to hit the ball. The Pitching Machine at 33 Feet drill on page 108 can help prepare players for such a situation. This is an effective drill that is easy to set up.

Several years ago, when we had a pitcher who could throw a 70 mph fastball, we played a very good team in the NCAA regional tournament. This team had no problem getting around on our pitcher early in the game. We were fortunate to win the game, and immediately afterward, we asked the opposing coach what his team had done to prepare. Here's what he said: "We put our machine at 33 feet and turned it up all the way. We hit that way all week."

Even when using front tosses, the tosser should throw at a speed that hitters will see in a real game. To do this, the tosser may have to shorten the distance to 20 feet or so. If hitters work regularly against pitches approximating what they will see from the best opponents, the hitters will learn to stay fundamentally strong against that speed and will be much more comfortable in those situations. The bottom line is that hitters must prepare to compete against the best in their league or conference. Increased bat speed gives them confidence and allows them to believe that they are prepared for any pitcher.

Some of the bat speed drills require specific equipment. Here are some descriptions that will be helpful in obtaining the necessary equipment:

- **Batting tube.** As shown in figure 6.2, this is an elongated rubber tube that can be purchased commercially.
- **Woofin speed stix.** This device (figure 6.3) is sold commercially by ProCut and can be purchased for players of all sizes and ages. A homemade version can also be created. For college players, a long thin piece of plastic PVC cut to a length of 45 inches (114 cm) will do. The stick is weighted on one end, and the weight is cemented firmly into the end of the PVC pipe. When swung, the stick makes a "woofin" sound. This sound is very similar to the sound made when swinging a bat with a chute on the end.
- **16-inch softballs.** These can be purchased commercially from most sporting goods stores or suppliers.
- **Weighted balls.** These can be purchased commercially. As noted in chapter 4, if you do not have access to weighted balls, you can take some really old softballs or baseballs, let them soak in a bucket of water for a

Figure 6.2   Batting tube.

Figure 6.3   Batter using a Woofin speed stix.

few days, and then let them dry in the sun.

- **Weighted bats.** Several types of end weights can be used on bats, and weighted bands can be placed on any bat at the bottom of the stem (figure 6.4). Screw-on weights of 8, 10, 12, and 14 ounces can also be purchased at almost any sporting goods store. Some players use baseball bats of higher weight and length or

Figure 6.4   Various bat weights.

wooden bats that have screw-in weights attached to the nub of the bat. In bat speed drills, the weight should be on the bottom end of the bat (commonly called the nub). Weight in the middle or on the barrel promotes casting or sweeping. Players must learn to keep their hands inside the ball, so they should practice with end weights.

PITCHING MACHINE AT 33 FEET

Purpose   This drill helps batters develop faster reaction time and improve their tracking ability.

Execution   Set the pitching machine 10 feet (3 m) closer than the regulation pitching distance used at the level of play for the batters. For college, 18U, and 16U players, regulation pitching distance is 43 feet (13.1 m), so the machine would be set at 33 feet (10.1 m) in this drill. Players take normal swings from this distance, working on speeding up the hands in order to react quickly and be on time at contact. Players should complete three sets of 15 repetitions.

Coaching Points   Initially, this drill may be very frustrating for batters. They will often be late and experience failure. Encourage them to stick with it. The batters will soon be able to hit the ball well from this short distance. The payoff will be the team's increased confidence when facing a faster pitcher.

HITTING TUBE

Purpose   This drill helps batters develop strength in the wrists, and it is a very effective drill for teaching batters to stay long on the ball.

Execution   In this drill, a batting tube hangs vertically in the batting cage at approximately the height of the strike zone. This height can easily be changed relative to the size of the batter. The batter takes a normal swing, striking the tube as if it were a softball (figure 6.5). The tube provides resistance when struck and forces the batter to drive through the solid object, much as she would drive through the ball. The goal is to keep the barrel moving when it strikes the tube, not allowing the resistance presented by the tube to stop the swing or cause a hesitation through contact and into the batter's finish. The tube will swing away from the batter when it is struck; it will then swing back like a pendulum. The batter steadies the tube for her next repetition. Players should complete three sets of 10 repetitions.

Figure 6.5   Batter swinging at tube.

Coaching Points   The Poor Man's Circuit in appendix B details a method for making a similar resistance tube using an old football tackling dummy.

Variation Several variations of this drill are easy to set up, and they provide the same results. Older readers may remember their parents or coaches hanging a tire from a tree. That is a good substitute, but the tire is more difficult to drive through and move because of the size. We know a coach who uses a tire on a pole that rotates when hit. This device is very effective and easy to make. The coach who created it is a very good hitting coach whose players have great bat speed.

WOOFIN STIX DRILL

Purpose This drill helps players strengthen their wrists and fast-twitch muscles. It is an excellent bat speed drill that can be used by players of all ages.

Execution The batter uses a woofin stix. She should perform the drill in an area (in the cage or on the field) that is large enough for her to swing the stick without hitting anyone or anything. There is no ball involved in this drill. The batter swings the woofin stix as if it were a bat, as fast as she can. As soon as she reaches the finish of her swing, she quickly brings the bat back on the same swing plane to the ready position, and then she immediately swings again. She does a set of 10 repetitions (regular swing and back is one repetition) with no pause between the repetitions. The batter does three sets of 10 repetitions with 30 seconds of rest between sets. The batter must swing hard throughout the drill.

Coaching Points Make sure that the batters' fundamentals are perfect. Batters should load, stride, and swing 10 times in succession with no pause in between the swings. They must finish the swing before bringing the bat back to the initial ready position. Batters must also make sure that the bat is brought back on the same swing plane. This will reinforce a level swing path to the ball. Batters will be sweating when they finish!

QUICK TOSS WITH WEIGHTED BALLS

Purpose This is a great drill for helping players increase bat speed and for getting the players' blood flowing. The weighted balls provide more resistance during the swing. This drill is tough and also serves as a conditioning drill. Players will be tired when finished, but they will be better hitters.

Execution In this drill, the coach sets up in a kneeling position 45 degrees in front of the batter. Five sets of four weighted balls are on the ground in front of the coach. The coach tosses four balls very quickly into the hitting zone. The batter must swing and reset for each ball. The batter rests for 10 seconds, and then the coach repeats the toss sequence. The batter must do five sets of four repetitions to complete the drill.

(continued)

Quick Toss With Weighted Balls *(continued)*

Coaching Points   As with all bat speed drills, the batter's fundamentals must be good. When players first start performing this drill, they may tend to loop on the backswing and begin to uppercut on the actual swing in an effort to hurry the swing so they complete the drill in tune with the toss. The coach needs to give the batters feedback during the drill and make sure they understand that each swing must be short and compact. With younger and less experienced players, the coach may have to take a little more time between tosses to give the batter time to finish the swing and reset. The coach doesn't want to go so fast that the batter breaks off her swing's finish in order to hurry and reset. At the same time, the batter's goal is to perform the swing and reset as fast as she can while not sacrificing any fundamentals.

Variation   When first starting this drill, especially with younger players, a coach may want to use regular softballs. As the players progress, the coach can switch to baseballs (this will also add a focus component to the drill). Finally, the coach can move to weighted softballs or baseballs.

TEE WITH WEIGHTED BALLS OR 16-INCH SOFTBALLS

Purpose   This drill helps players develop wrist and forearm strength in order to increase bat speed.

Execution   Using either a 16-inch softball or a weighted ball that is 12 inches or larger, the batter takes swings off a batting tee, hitting into a portable backstop (see figure 6.6). This drill is often performed in a batting cage. The larger or weighted ball will create resistance for the batter and force her to drive through the ball at contact in order to hit it solidly, much like in the Hitting Tube drill on page 108. Players complete two sets of 10 repetitions.

Figure 6.6   Drill setup.

Coaching Points   The batters should be working on bat speed while still maintaining a correct contact point and proper swing fundamentals. Make sure the resistance of the ball does not stop the batter's swing. The batter must push through at contact and stay long into her finish.

HIGH TEE, WEIGHTED BATS, AND WEIGHTED BALLS

Purpose   In this drill, batters use weighted bats and balls, which helps them develop strength and increase bat speed. The high tee forces the batter to keep her hands up and maintain good swing fundamentals, and it helps the batter work on loft to get distance. This is an advanced drill that can be used daily by college-level players. The drill can be used at any level. However, we would discourage the use of weighted bats or balls with players who are 12 and under.

Execution   The tee is positioned at the height of the batter's chest. With a weighted ball on the tee, the batter takes normal swings into a net using a weighted bat. The weighted bat and balls help the batter develop strength and increase bat speed, while the high tee forces the batter to keep her hands up and maintain good swing fundamentals. The batter completes 3 sets of 10 repetitions.

Coaching Points   In addition to working on bat speed, the batters should be continually reinforcing muscle memory relative to the position of the hands throughout the swing. When first starting to use this drill or any variations of the drill, batters should start with lighter bats and lighter weights; they can then work up to heavier weights as bat speed increases. Younger players should use smaller bats to hit off the high tee.

Variation   A variation of this drill is to do repetitions with one arm. The batter can start by doing a couple sets of forearm swings and then switch to backhand swings. The batter should also start with a lighter bat and then work up to a heavier bat. One-arm drills really strengthen the batter's wrists and are a big part of our bat speed program.

THROWING BATS

Purpose　This is a multipurpose drill. The drill helps the batter increase bat speed because it strengthens her wrists and forearms. It also helps the batter learn to keep the barrel of the bat in the zone as long as possible. Many top-level teams use this drill on a regular basis.

Execution　This drill requires 10 to 12 old bats that can no longer be used in a game or practice. The drill can be done in a cage with a reinforced catch net, but it is more effective on the dirt portion of the field. (Of course, throwing bats into the grass outfield may create divots and upset the groundskeeper.) The player performing the drill stands at home plate or a few feet behind home plate with a bucket containing the old bats.

Figure 6.7　Throwing bats in action.

The player grabs a bat and then loads, strides, and throws the bat as far as she can up the middle of the field, targeting the pitcher's mound (figure 6.7). Each player should do three sets of 10 throws.

Coaching Points　The player should work to stay long through the swing and keep the barrel in the zone as long as possible. Make sure that players extend their hands toward the pitcher before releasing the bat. A player throwing the bat to the left is a direct indication that she is pulling out. Most players throw the bat to their pull field when they first attempt this drill. Make sure the player doesn't slow down her swing to direct the bat up the middle. She should swing hard, as if she were hitting a ball, and release the bat where contact would be made. With practice the player will learn to swing hard and throw the bat up the middle.

CHAPTER 7

Offensive Strategies

Offensive strategies are developed and perfected in practice, beginning in the off-season and continuing through preseason. Once the season begins, the coach should set aside time in each practice for the team to work on one or two of these strategies. The strategies outlined in this chapter are really a game within a game and can be thought of as similar to the special teams in football. They are employed to increase the team's ability to score runs and to keep the defense off balance. Most important, they require specific skills and total attention to the game situation.

In this chapter, we discuss several strategies that can be used at all levels of the game. All of these strategies can help a team become a greater offensive threat. Some of these strategies require speed, and some require specific placement of the ball. Every offensive strategy requires prepitch evaluations, knowledge of the opponent's strengths and weaknesses, and a commitment to excellence. Each strategy is most effective in specific situations. Coaches and players need to know when, why, and how to use the strategies. This is discussed in detail in the chapter, and drills are provided that can be used to perfect each strategy.

We constantly encourage our players to play smarter, not just harder. We want them to be mentally in the game at all times and to expect the unexpected. The skills required to execute the strategies in this chapter will make players better in all facets of the offensive game and will even help them on defense. In learning how to perfect these strategies offensively, the players will also learn how to defend them. Successful execution of one or more of these plays in a game not only increases the team's ability to score but also fires up a team and gets players excited.

ANALYZING THE OPPONENT

Knowledge of the opponent's strengths and weaknesses is critical in deciding when to call a certain play or initiate an offensive strategy. Percentages always play a key role in the success factor of any play. In the best possible scenario, the coach and players would know the arm strength, arm accuracy, and range of the opponent's defensive players. They would know the catcher's blocking and throwing abilities and how she leads and directs the team as a field general. They especially need to know a lot about the pitcher, including how she fields, how she throws overhand, and how she reacts to the unexpected. Knowing what the pitcher throws in certain situations, especially when behind in the count or when needing a strikeout, is very important. Other useful information about the pitcher includes how often her pitches are in the dirt and whether she turns her back on runners in scoring position. The bottom line is that the more a team knows about the opponent, the better the team's chances of properly executing an offensive strategy.

PITCH AWARENESS AND SELECTION

An often overlooked factor in offensive softball is pitch awareness and pitch selection. Pitch selection is very important in every at-bat, but it is even more important when executing offensive strategies such as the suicide squeeze, hit-and-run, sacrifice fly, and first-and-third play. In several of these strategies, the batter needs the count in her favor in order to dictate a certain type of pitch and to avoid the pitchout. Of course, batters always want to work the count to their favor even if a special play is not on. But with the special play on, the batter is trying to increase the chances of getting the type of pitch that will enable her to execute the play.

Specific strategies are discussed in the Special Offensive Strategies section on page 116, and the optimum pitch situation for each strategy is provided. One thing we teach our players is that on-base percentage is more important than batting average. We also constantly coach them on swinging at their pitch and not swinging at junk. Many studies have shown that a batter ahead in the count has a much better chance of getting a hit than a batter behind in the count. Simply said, either the pitcher controls the plate, or the batter controls the plate. One of my favorite quotes is from hall of famer Rogers Hornsby, who said, "When I get in the batter's box, I feel sorry for the pitcher."

READING THE DEFENSE

Players and coaches must be sure to read the defense before each pitch. The offense needs to know the position and alignment of the outfield. What is the outfielders' depth and are they shaded left or right? The offense must also read the infield, checking the position of the corners and middle infield. Are the corners in and guarding the line? Who is covering each base? Is the shortstop deep in the hole? If so, this indicates that the third-base player will cover third on the steal and that the second-base player will cover second. Is the second-base player shading toward second to discourage the steal or the double steal of second and home? Does the catcher drop to her knees on the low pitch with runners on base? Is the catcher quick and adept at covering the area in front of the plate?

The defense will provide clues that help the offense execute the special plays discussed throughout the rest of this chapter. Be alert and focused. Study the defense and know the situation before each pitch. Coaches should be sure to have a "wipe-off" signal to cancel the play if the defense suddenly shifts to a more advantageous position to defend the play. Generating runs through the use of these offensive strategies is an ongoing game of cat and mouse. Pitch count and defensive positioning as well as sudden defensive awareness directly influence the offensive team's chances of success.

FIELD AND WEATHER CONDITIONS

Field and weather conditions affect the speed game, which includes all phases of baserunning, bunting, slapping, and stealing. The firmness of the playing field has a direct impact on the slap game, first-and-third situations, and the team's ability to steal a base. For a slapper, a hard field will play fast and is therefore conducive to a hard slap through the infield or a chop slap that bounces high. A bunt or soft slap may not be the best weapon because a hard surface will allow the ball to reach the fielder quickly. Conversely, a soft field or one that is moist from a recent rain will not play as fast. In that case, a bunt or soft slap is the better choice. For base runners, a firm surface allows for better footing, so runners have a greater chance of success when stealing than they would on a softer field. Coaches and players need to analyze the conditions, especially the bounce of the ball and the footing between the bases.

SPECIAL OFFENSIVE STRATEGIES

Several plays or strategies can be put into an offensive game plan to help the team achieve success. A team must devote sufficient practice time to the execution of these strategies. A play will likely fail if players are not confident in their ability to execute it, regardless of the weakness and susceptibility in the defense. There is nothing like practice to achieve the level of confidence necessary to be successful.

This section discusses the following strategies:

- Taking control of the batter's box
- Knowing when to attack or work the count
- Sacrifice bunt
- Push bunt
- Bunt-and-run
- Slap-and-run
- First-and-third play
- Double steal
- Stealing home
- Hit-and-run
- Sacrifice fly
- Hitting behind the runner
- Hitting to the opposite field

Taking Control of the Batter's Box

Every at-bat is a constant battle of wits and ability that the batter must control if she wants to be successful. The batter's box is softball's version of a battle zone. It is a line of demarcation that can only be controlled by one person. Three different players are engaged in trying to gain control of the 7-by-3-foot piece of softball real estate. Those players are the pitcher, the catcher, and the batter. Either the pitcher and catcher or the batter will prevail. Each has a strategy that she hopes will help her win the at-bat.

Softball is a game of adjustment. It is also a game of studying and adapting to change. Batters must have a good idea of what the pitcher will throw in certain situations. They need to know the pitcher's speed, movement, and what pitch she will likely go to in various counts, especially with two strikes. Batters also need to know if the pitcher is primarily a curve and screwball pitcher or a drop and rise ball pitcher—or if she throws all of those pitches. Most important, the batter must know if the pitcher has a good off-speed pitch and how often she uses it. Before the batter enters the box, she should have a plan of where she will stand in the box. She should also have the ability to adjust in the box depending on the count and what she has observed during the at-bat. Here are a few general rules:

- If the pitcher is throwing slow and low, the batter should move up in the box; her back foot should be even with the front of the plate.
- If the pitcher is throwing fast with no movement, the batter should get as far back in the box as possible in order to give herself more time.
- If the pitcher is throwing hard with movement, the batter should get up in the box and try to catch the pitch before it moves.
- If the pitcher is consistently pitching away from the batter, the batter should crowd the plate. If the batter is being consistently jammed, she should back off the plate.
- With two strikes, the batter should get closer to the plate and shorten her swing to make better contact. The batter should also train herself to foul off close pitches that she does not want when she has two strikes.

Practice   The Pitch Recognition drill described in chapter 4 on page 75 is a great drill for working on stance adjustments in the batter's box. The batter stands in while the pitchers are going through their bullpen workouts. The batter should vary her positioning in the box. She should stand in the front, in the back, crowding the plate, and off the plate. The batter must learn to see pitches from these different perspectives, and she should make note of which type of pitches she sees more clearly from the various box positions.

Knowing When to Attack or Work the Count

For a team to be successful offensively, one of the most important offensive statistics is on-base percentage. When discussing offensive strategies, a coach must talk about on-base percentages, the count on the batter at the time a special play is called, and the impact of a base on balls. For example, the whole purpose of the sacrifice bunt is to advance the runner. When this play is on, the batter wants to be disciplined and bunt only strikes. If the pitcher doesn't throw strikes, the batter should be patient and take the walk. A base on balls advances the runner, puts the batter on base, and does not cost the team an out. When the count is in the batter's favor, the team has a much better chance of executing a special play and scoring a run.

Hitters must learn to swing at their pitch, to go deep in the count, and to avoid swinging at pitches designed to make them chase outside the strike zone. Those pitches decrease a hitter's opportunity to be successful. The best hitters are usually the same hitters who have a high on-base percentage and draw a lot of bases on balls. Batters need to be mentally ready to attack their pitch when it comes. To be ready, the batter should assume that every pitch thrown will be her pitch.

During the pitcher's motion, the batter should think *yes, yes, yes.* Then, if the pitch is truly a good one, the batter is ready to swing hard and attack the ball. If the pitch is not one that the batter wants, she lets it go. It is easy for a batter to go from a "yes, yes, yes" approach to "no" when the pitch is not one that she wants to swing at. However, if a batter is thinking *no, no, no* or *maybe* during the pitcher's delivery, the batter will be unable to get ready to swing in time (she only has a fraction of a second) if she realizes it's a good pitch to hit. By studying the pitcher from the dugout and the on-deck circle, batters will have a pretty good idea of whether she throws first-pitch strikes or tries to get the batter to chase early. Batters want the count in their favor, and the coach wants the count in the batter's favor before calling the offensive strategies outlined in this chapter.

Practice Several drills—including the Hit-and-Run, Favorite Pitch, and Two Strikes drills that follow—can be used in batting practice sessions to give batters an opportunity to work on various counts. These drills will help batters learn when to attack versus when to go deep in the count. The Hit-and-Run drill is great for teaching aggressiveness. Next, players should move on to the Favorite Pitch drill, which teaches patience. A great former major leaguer recently said, "Too many hitters are in a hurry to make outs early in the count. The great hitters are patient enough to wait for the pitcher to make a mistake." Finally, the Two Strikes drill helps batters understand the strike zone and learn plate discipline.

HIT-AND-RUN

Purpose   This drill gets batters into an aggressive mind-set.

Execution   This drill is most effective off of live pitching, but may also use front toss with a screen. In this drill, the batter swings at any pitch regardless of whether it is in the strike zone. The drill simulates a hit-and-run call during a game where the base runner is stealing and the batter must swing at the pitch. The batter needs to use a "yes, yes, yes" mentality because the decision on ball or strike is out of her hands. She must hit each pitch. The batter completes five at-bats in the drill.

Coaching Points   It is amazing to watch how batters are able to put great swings on bad pitches when they are mentally aggressive.

FAVORITE PITCH

Purpose   This drill teaches batters to be patient and wait for their pitch.

Execution   This drill uses live pitching. The batter should be mentally locked into the part of the strike zone where her favorite pitch is located and should be ready to attack any pitch thrown there. She lets all other pitches go, even if they are strikes. This drill simulates what batters need to do in hitters' counts (0-0, 1-0, 2-0, 2-1, 3-1) and maybe even until they get two strikes. The batter completes five at-bats in the drill.

Coaching Points   Batters who are patient and wait for the pitcher to make a mistake in their favorite zone are usually successful. The batter's mindset is very important. There is a big difference between focusing on her zone and attacking the pitch and focusing on not swinging at pitches outside her favorite zone. Anytime a hitter thinks about what not to do, she is less aggressive. The batter must trust that if she is patient the pitcher will eventually make a mistake in her zone.

TWO STRIKES

Purpose   This drill enables batters to practice being in a two-strike count.

Execution   This drill uses live pitching. The batter starts this drill with a two-strike count, so she has to swing at every pitch in the strike zone, even if the pitch is not her particular strength. For the batter, this is the difference between being aggressive in *her* zone (a hitter's count) and aggressive in *the* zone (a pitcher's count). The batter completes five at-bats starting with a two-strike count each time.

(continued)

Two Strikes *(continued)*

Coaching Points Batters must understand that having two strikes doesn't mean they swing all out at everything. They should still make the pitcher throw strikes. Some people describe a batter's strategy with two strikes as protecting the plate. We don't like to use the word *protect* because its connotation puts the batter in a defensive mind-set. The batter should remain aggressive when she swings, but she must have a good understanding of the zone and make good decisions on balls and strikes.

Sacrifice Bunt

The sacrifice bunt is an extremely important offensive strategy, especially in a tight game with two outstanding pitchers on the mound. The object of this strategy is to sacrifice the batter in order to move the runner. Simply said, the coach is willing to give up an out to put the runner in scoring position. This strategy also allows the coach to ensure that the team's best RBI hitters come to the plate with runners in scoring position. The first goal for the batter is to bunt strikes. This is important for two reasons: (1) The pitcher is not going to groove a pitch in this situation, and (2) a base on balls advances the runner without a sacrifice.

Many bunters chase the first pitch, which is usually out of the zone, and pop it up, sometimes causing the runner to get doubled off and thus ending a promising inning. The batter must realize that she is a sacrificial lamb in this situation and is not expected to get on base. The batter must simply get the ball down. She should use the sacrifice bunting technique outlined in chapter 1. To increase the chances of getting the bunt down in fair territory, the batter makes sure that she is up in the box and that she squares around a little early. Her feet should be still. The cue "feet in concrete" can be used to emphasize that the batter's feet should not be moving until the bunt is down. Another way to reinforce this is by teaching sacrifice bunters to "appreciate, then accelerate." In a sacrifice situation, the batter should pause and appreciate her terrific bunt before she runs to first base. This will help keep her feet still at contact. Most problems occur when the bunter gets anxious, starts moving in the box, and swings at a bad pitch, especially a high pitch.

Practice The sacrifice bunt is a technique that a team needs to practice so that every player can lay down a sacrifice bunt when called on to do so. A coach should teach the sacrifice bunting technique provided in chapter 1 at the beginning of the season. Using the drills outlined in chapter 1, batters can learn to bunt by progressing from bunting off a front toss with Wiffle balls, to bunting off a machine, and finally to executing sacrifice bunts off live pitching. Coaches should make sure that a batter's fundamentals are good before she progresses. Using cones or chalk to outline target areas where the bunts should land is a great way to teach the sacrifice bunt. Incorporate live bunting drills into each practice. Videotape the bunters and let them observe their progress. Video provides excellent feedback, and feedback is "the breakfast of champions."

Push Bunt

When using the push bunt, the batter's goal is to prevent the hard-charging defense from getting the lead runner at second base. Pushing the bunt by first or third base into the outfield may allow the lead runner to go all the way to third base. Further, successful execution of a push bunt tends to keep the corners back in a bunt situation for the rest of the game. This increases the chances of a successful execution of the sacrifice bunt.

The push bunt is a very effective offensive strategy and can be used when the corner players are expecting the bunt and are charging quickly. As mentioned in chapter 1, correct execution of this play can result in defensive chaos—the ball could reach the outfield, evading hard-charging corners and middle infielders who are rushing to cover first base and second base.

Practice   The push bunt is a repetition skill. Players should practice this skill using the progression of bunting drills outlined in chapter 1, including push bunting off a front toss (using Wiffle balls), push bunting off a machine, and push bunting off live pitching. Cones should be placed farther away from home plate to emphasize that this bunt needs to be pushed farther away from the plate than a sacrifice bunt. A lot of repetition is required to perfect this skill; most batters tend to miss the ball or pop it up when first learning how to push bunt. This is also a skill that should be videotaped in order to provide feedback to the player.

Bunt-and-Run

The goal of the bunt-and-run strategy is to move the lead runner into scoring position without sacrificing an out. The batter takes a normal batting stance and does not show bunt until the last possible moment. The batter merely slides her hands up on the bat, executes a crossover step with the back foot, and taps the pitch toward the least defended corner as she is running out of the box. The main difference between this tactic and the slap is the surprise factor—the batter is trying to catch the corners off guard.

The bunt-and-run is usually most successful when the defensive players, especially the corners, are playing back and do not expect a bunt. This is a tactic that right-handed batters will use more than lefties, because corners tend to play back on them more than they do on the left-handed batters. The bunt-and-run needs to be initiated with a positive pitch count, because this tactic has a better chance of succeeding when it is a surprise to the defense. Any player with good speed can execute a bunt-and-run. The key is the position of the third- and first-base players just before the pitch.

A variation of this play is the sacrifice bunt-and-run. The difference here is that the batter is not necessarily trying to bunt for a base hit; however, the runner is going on the pitch, so the batter must be sure to get the bunt down. This strategy is useful when the corners are expecting the bunt and are playing in so that they can try to force the out at second base. By putting the base runner on the move when the pitch is thrown, the offense can avoid the force. The risk, however, is that the batter will pop up the bunt or miss the ball. For this play, the batter should be in a hitter's count. In addition, the coach should make sure that the team has a batter at the plate who is confident in her ability to get the bunt down on any pitch thrown.

Practice   Live batting practice is the best way to practice the bunt-and-run. A team should practice this play both with the corners playing back and with them crowding the batter. Batters need to become comfortable bunting with the corners playing in on them.

Slap-and-Run

This strategy is very similar to the bunt-and-run. The runner is going on the pitch, and the slapper must get the ball on the ground to protect the runner. A team would normally use this strategy when the runner on first base does not have much speed and would not be able to steal. On this play, the slapper must put the ball on the ground or the runner will be out at second on the throw from the catcher. Like the bunt-and-run, this is a good strategy to use to move a slower runner into scoring position. And if the play is executed perfectly, the offense will catch the defense by surprise and have two on and nobody out.

We have two signals that we use when a slapper is at the plate with a runner on first: One signal indicates that the slapper should move the runner using the slap-and-run; the other indicates that the slapper should read the defense and identify which skill (bunt, soft slap, or hard slap) will most likely avoid a force-out at second base. Again, the main factors in calling the slap-and-run are the speed of the runner on base and the slapper's ability to get the ball on the ground with the runner on the move. This is another strategy that works best with a positive pitch count.

Practice   Set up live situations with the infield defense, a runner on first, and a slapper at the plate. Vary the coverage at second on the steal by having both the shortstop and the second-base player cover at different times. Also vary the speed of the runners at first. When the runner at first has average speed, the slapper executes a slap-and-run, understanding that she must swing at any pitch thrown and must get the ball on the ground (or at least foul it off to protect the runner). When the runner has above-average speed, the slapper reads the coverage and decides which option is best.

Remember, in this situation, the runner is not going on the pitch, so the batter doesn't have to swing. Rather, the batter is looking for a pitch that will enable her to successfully execute the skill. If the second-base player is covering on the steal and the shortstop is playing in the 5-6 hole, a hard slap to third or short will likely force the runner at second. In this case, a bunt may be a better choice. If the shortstop is covering second on the steal, she may have to cheat toward the bag and away from the 5-6 hole. A soft slap in the 5-6 hole is an excellent option in that situation.

Offensive First-and-Third Play

The toughest play to execute offensively is the first-and-third play. This play and the suicide squeeze are two of the most exciting and rewarding strategies. In the first-and-third play, the goal is to have the runner on first base steal second and to have the runner on third base steal home. This play is used to score a run from third when the team is having difficulty scoring off a really good pitcher. The coach must make sure that the runners and the batter know that the play is on. The batter must protect the runners and hinder the catcher by swinging through at the pitch. This play requires very good baserunning instincts and excellent sliding techniques.

The first-and-third play can be initiated with a straight steal or a delayed steal. The type of steal usually depends on the speed of the runners at both first and third. The optimum situation for this play is to have fast runners on both first and third, but the play can work if only the runner at third is fast. In a straight steal, the runner on first base breaks hard for second base. If the throw comes through to second, the runner slides into the front side of the bag to block the shortstop from throwing home and to allow the run to score. In the delayed steal, the runner goes half speed to second, hoping to get caught in a rundown that would allow the runner on third to score. In either case, the runner on third base takes a lead and breaks for home if the throw goes through. If the throw is cut, the runner returns to third. In this scenario, a run does not score, but two runners are now in scoring position.

Practice   The first-and-third play must be practiced on a regular basis. We have scored many runs on this play. In practice, set up this situation using an infield defense and base runners rotating in at first and third (see figure 7.1). Runners should mix things up by using both straight and delayed steals to second. Practicing this play is a great way to teach base runners to read the defense and to execute appropriate slides into the bases. The defense also gets the best practice possible on defending the first-and-third play.

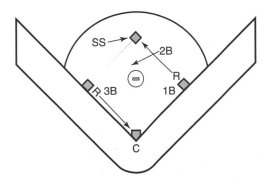

Figure 7.1   Infield and base runners.

Double Steal

The double steal is similar to the first-and-third play, except in this case, the base runners are on first base and second base, and the object is to advance them to second and third. This strategy works best with a speedy runner on second base. The trail runner on first base does not have to be fast, but she must be a good base runner. The key here is the steal of third. As any coach knows, third base is stolen off the shortstop. Successful execution of this play moves two base runners into immediate scoring position without sacrificing an out.

The right time to implement this strategy is when the coach observes the shortstop too deep in the 5-6 hole to beat the runner on second to third base. The coach calls for a fake bunt and steal. The batter waits until the last possible moment to show bunt. This draws the third-base player in to cover the bunt and creates a footrace to third between the shortstop and the base runner. With the shortstop covering, the base runner should slide to the home plate side of third base, giving her a better chance to evade the tag if the throw and the shortstop both get there on time. The runner from second needs to read the third-base player as she takes off. If the third-base player does not take the fake, the runner aborts the play and returns to second. The trail runner coming from first base needs to keep her eyes on the lead runner in case the fake bunt does not work. This is a risky but rewarding play.

Practice   To practice this play, place runners at first and second base with an infield defense in position; new runners rotate in after each play. A batter is in the box to execute the fake bunt. The runners take off on the release of the pitch to home. The runner on second must sprint hard off the bag toward third and must read the third-base player while still going hard. If the third-base player bites on the batter's fake bunt, the runner continues to third, and the trail runner steals second. If the third-base player doesn't bite on the fake, the runner puts on the brakes and returns to second base. The runner at second doesn't need to worry about a pickoff because the shortstop will be breaking to third to cover the steal and the second-base player will be breaking to first to cover on the perceived bunt.

Stealing Home

This is another very risky play—so risky, in fact, that only one runner in the major leagues stole home during the 2009 season. That player was Jacoby Ellsbury of the Boston Red Sox. His steal was shown over and over on ESPN because of the rarity of the play. Stealing home is also a rare play in softball, but because the distance between third base and home plate is shorter in softball, it happens more often.

The runner steals home off the catcher and pitcher. The offense must study both before initiating this play. Does the catcher look at the runner on third base before she throws back to the pitcher? Does the pitcher look at the runner on third base as she receives the ball? Does the pitcher turn her back on the runner? Is the third-base player attentive to the runner on third base? All of these factors determine whether a steal will be successful.

This information needs to be gathered long before trying to steal home. From the first inning on, watch the exchange between the pitcher and catcher whenever runners are on base. Are they alert to the runners? Do they get lax as the game goes on? Does the pitcher get frustrated and lose focus after a base on balls or a base hit? This play will likely only work once in a game, so it must be planned and set up well. Another key is for the base runner to look relaxed on the pitches before she attempts the steal so that she lulls the defense into thinking she isn't a threat to go. To execute the play, the runner takes a short walking lead from third before the catcher returns the ball to the pitcher. If the catcher does not look at the runner, the runner breaks *the instant* the catcher releases the throw to the pitcher. The runner should slide to the back of the plate.

Practice   A great time to work on this play is during live scrimmage situations in team practices. This work will also help keep the team's own pitchers and catchers alert to the delayed steal. The coach should tell the base runners to look early for opportunities to catch the battery off guard; the runners try to determine if the opening is there. The runners should attempt the delayed steal when they see an opportunity.

Hit-and-Run

The hit-and-run is a strategy that is as old as the game. Simply said, the runner is going on the pitch, and the batter must make contact with the ball. The batter is trying to hit the ball on the ground and, if possible, hit behind the runner. This is definitely a strategy that requires a positive pitch count—that is, the pitcher is behind in the count and needs to throw a strike. The hit-and-run is usually used in lieu of the steal, because of the runner's foot speed, but it can be used with a runner of any speed. To have a good chance of successfully executing this play, the batter must be a contact hitter who can put the ball in play (or at least foul it off if the pitch is in on the batter).

By starting the runner on the hit-and-run, the coach is trying to move the runner from first to third or even from second to the plate on the hit. If the pitcher, the catcher, or the opposing coach expects this play, the opponents could call a pitchout. If that occurs, the batter must reach across the plate or up and away and at least foul off the ball. The hit-and-run is an excellent offensive strategy and should be practiced often. Much like the suicide squeeze (see chapter 1), this play can jump-start a team and change the momentum of the game. Also like the suicide squeeze, this play requires a very savvy and trustworthy batter at the plate. Our teams have used the hit-and-run and the squeeze numerous times to score runs and win games. For these plays to be effective, they must be a normal part of the team's offense, and the players must feel comfortable executing them.

Practice   Incorporate the Hit-and-Run drill on page 119 into the team's batting practice workouts. This will help the batters become comfortable and confident hitting any pitch thrown at them. Base runners can also be included in the drill. The key for the runner is to take off hard—as if stealing—and to find the ball *without slowing down* when it is put in play. If the batter hits a line drive, the runner should keep going; if the line drive is caught in the infield, the runner has no chance of getting back in time anyway. The only time the runner stops and retreats is if the batter hits a pop-up or fly ball. In this case, the runner will likely have time to return safely to the bag.

Runners tend to make two mistakes on this play. First, they don't run hard off the bag on the pitch; instead, they jog and wait to see what type of hit occurs. Second, they stop or pause at contact to see what the batter did. Both mistakes defeat the purpose of the hit-and-run, which is to try to advance the runner two bases instead of just one. When calling this play, the coach should take responsibility for the possibility of the runner getting doubled off on a line-drive out—and should make sure the runners understand that. The runners should know that their job is to run hard and execute the play properly from the start.

Sacrifice Fly

The sacrifice fly is an important strategy for moving the runners and especially for scoring a runner from third base. It can only occur with less than two outs. A good coach will teach the importance of being able to hit a sacrifice fly, which is more difficult than it might seem. Hitting a sacrifice fly requires a strong mental approach, a certain type of swing, and a good pitch count. When a batter hits a sacrifice fly that scores a runner from third, the batter earns an RBI, and the play does not count as an official at-bat.

Pitch selection is extremely important. Pitchers are taught to keep the ball down in a sacrifice fly situation. The ideal pitch for the pitcher would be low and in or low and away. The ideal pitch for the batter would be a pitch above the waist. The batter must not get overanxious and swing at a bad first pitch. She should get set in the box, preferably in the front of the box, and work the count. When she gets her pitch, she should attack the ball with a slight uppercut swing.

Practice   In batting practice sessions, batters should take repetitions where the goal is a sacrifice fly. In a round of 20 cuts, a batter could devote 5 to sacrifice flies. The batter should swing at pitches up in the zone that she can lift to the outfield; she should take low pitches that will likely result in ground balls.

Hitting Behind the Runner

The purpose of hitting behind the runner is to avoid the double play with a runner on first base. If the batter can successfully execute this strategy, she increases the base runner's chances of going from first base to third base. When the batter hits behind the runner on first base (see figure 7.2), the defense is required to make a much more difficult throw from the outfield, and in softball, this almost always requires a cut play. To hit behind the runner, a right-handed batter must let the pitch come farther into the strike zone and then drive the ball into right field. A left-handed batter needs to look for an inside or middle-in pitch and drive it in the 3-4 hole.

Practice   Hitting behind the runner is an important skill that every player needs to learn. It is a skill that requires repetition during daily hitting drills. This technique requires patience and practice. During batting practice, batters should devote a round or a number of swings to executing this skill. For these swings, batters swing at the pitches that help them hit the ball to right field (outside pitches for right-handed batters and inside pitches for left-handed batters). These types of drills help batters become better at understanding pitch selection and how to control their swings in order to hit balls to different fields.

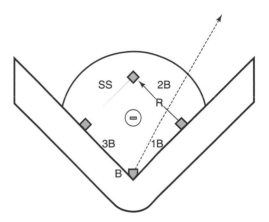

Figure 7.2   Paths for the runner and hit.

Hitting to the Opposite Field

This strategy is related to hitting behind the runner. Most young players do not have the patience or bat control to hit to the opposite field. Pitchers will try to work a good hitter, especially a power hitter, with pitches that are low and away. This pitching strategy is designed to negate the power swing and get the batter to swing at a pitch that gives her a lower chance of success. Batters who try to pull low and away pitches don't have much success and usually end up hitting weak ground balls. Both left- and right-handed batters need to practice hitting pitches in the outside part of the zone and even a ball off the plate. By doing this, they will hit to the opposite field, improve their individual performance, and help their team in advancing runners and scoring runs.

Practice Hitting to the opposite field is a skill that must be practiced to be mastered. Strategically place cones in the alleys in left center field and right center field. Batters should work on hitting outside pitches into those gaps. The batters can begin by hitting off a batting tee. This will help them understand where the contact point needs to be in order to hit an outside pitch solidly to the opposite field. The contact point will be deeper than it is when hitting an inside or middle pitch. Batters can then progress to hitting pitches delivered via a front toss to the outside part of the strike zone.

A competitive drill for working on hitting to the opposite field is the No Pop, No Pull drill from chapter 4 (on page 85). Give each batter 10 swings. The goal is to hit every ball swung at on a line (no pop) and to the opposite field (no pull). The batter gets a point for accomplishing both goals. Batters can compete with each other in this drill. Remember, practice breeds confidence, and confidence breeds success.

CHAPTER 8

Playing Within Your Team

All coaches have a philosophy about how they want to play the game. Offensively, some like to be very aggressive, while others are more conservative. Some like their hitters to attack the pitcher early in the count; others like their hitters to be more patient and work long at-bats. Some coaches prefer power hitting and playing for the game-breaking home run, while others prefer to generate runs by consistently pressuring the defense with speed. One thing, however, is true for all coaches: Great coaches are able to adapt their philosophy to the talent on their team.

OFFENSIVE PHILOSOPHY

We have already discussed the positive impact that both speed and power can have in creating an offense that generates a lot of runs. Ideally, a team's offense will have a mixture of speed and power so that the team can score runs in various ways. This is called "having a lot of tools in your toolbox." If you open a carpenter's toolbox, you won't see just one tool. You will find multiple tools because the carpenter never knows what challenges a job will present; the carpenter must be prepared to handle a variety of situations.

Similarly, a coach and team will face many situations during the course of a season—various field conditions, opponents with various strengths and weaknesses, pitching styles, umpires, weather conditions, and injuries, to name a few. The circumstances on a given day may determine whether the team plays small ball and capitalizes on its speed and short-game abilities, brings out the power hitters to smash home runs, or uses a mixture of both. In the ideal world, a coach has players who possess speed and power and can choose how to use these skills depending on the opponent and conditions.

Most coaches, however, live in the real world and don't have every tool available to them. Therefore, they must ensure that the team's players play within their abilities. The speedy slapper isn't going to have a lot of success if she is asked to hit home runs; the slow but strong power hitter will often fail if she is asked to slap her way on base and steal once she gets there. Great coaches put their players in a position to be successful.

This doesn't mean that coaches shouldn't have an offensive philosophy and approach that they try to get their team to play within as much as possible. Coaches who have the opportunity to recruit players to their team will undoubtedly select those who fit within their offensive system. For example, we like to have two or three speed players (players who can drag bunt, slap, and steal a lot of bases) in our lineup, and we direct our recruiting efforts accordingly. But even in the college game, where coaches have the opportunity to recruit, coaches sometimes need to adjust their approach to fit the talent available to them. In some recruiting years, speed players are not in abundance, or the quality of those available simply doesn't meet our needs. We learned a lesson one year when we made the mistake of taking the "best available" speed player in a class that didn't have great speed players. This player wasn't a strong enough offensive threat to crack our lineup. In the end, we had wasted valuable scholarship money on a player who couldn't help us on the field. In hindsight, we should have recruited a power hitter and used a more power-laden lineup until great speed players emerged in the succeeding recruiting classes.

On the high school level, where coaches generally can't recruit their players, a coach must be open to changing her offensive philosophy every year if necessary to maximize the talent on the roster. This is not always easy to do because it requires the coach to be adept at learning more parts of the game. The coach must become comfortable not only with teaching the skills involved, but also with employing the game strategies necessary to score runs with those skills. Having said that, here's one strategy we would use if we were coaching softball players of high school age or younger: *run, run, run, run, and run some more!* Any player who possessed above-average speed would steal bases almost every time she got on base. And if the catcher was weak, we would even run players with average speed.

We believe that this is a sound strategy because in 20-plus years of coaching softball, we have been continually amazed at how few players are good at the most basic skills in softball: throwing and catching the ball. And it seems to get worse every year. If players struggle to throw and catch proficiently during warm-up and practice, consider how much more they may struggle when trying to perform these skills in a game with the pressure on. In the 2011 NCAA tournament—which includes the 64 teams involved in regionals, super regionals, and the Women's College World Series (theoretically, the best 64 teams in NCAA Division I)—runners were successful stealing bases at a .825 clip (231 stolen bases out of 280 attempts). If teams at the highest level of collegiate softball can steal successfully that often against some of the best catchers, it's safe to presume that the success rate in high school and younger age groups would be at least as high if not higher.

EVALUATE STRENGTHS AND WEAKNESSES

Within the first few practices, the coach should evaluate the strengths and weaknesses of the team. What does the team do well? What does the team struggle with? The coach can assess the team's skills using the categories of great, good, average, and poor. Figure 8.1 on page 132 provides a sample form for assessing a team's strengths and weaknesses.

The coach must then decide how to best spend the team's limited amount of practice time. The first priority should be to make the team's strengths great and to build a strategy around what the team does best. Maybe the team has strong pitching and defense but struggles offensively. In this case, the team should spend practice time perfecting the pitching and defense and building an offense that will manufacture a couple of runs each game. Although all coaches want to turn their team's weaknesses into strengths, coaches should

Figure 8.1 Team Characteristics for Assessment

Characteristics	Great	Good	Average	Poor	Comments
PITCHING					
Speed					
Control					
Movement					
Fielding ability					
CATCHING					
Arm strength					
Arm accuracy					
Release time					
Framing					
Blocking					
Fielding					
Softball IQ					
INFIELD DEFENSE					
Arm strength					
Arm accuracy					
Fielding ability					
Range					
Bunt defense					
Slap defense					
Softball IQ					
OUTFIELD DEFENSE					
Arm strength					
Arm accuracy					
Fielding ability					
Range					
Softball IQ					
TEAM SPEED					
HITTING					
For average					
For power					
SHORT GAME					
Bunting					
Slapping					
ATTITUDE					
TOUGHNESS					
COMPETITIVENESS					

From R. Weekly and K. Weekly, 2012, *High-scoring softball* (Champaign, IL: Human Kinetics).

first work to turn the team's good characteristics into great characteristics. Coaches shouldn't get so caught up in trying to improve the weaknesses that they ignore the team's strongest assets and the traits that will define the team's identity. The team's strengths will ultimately lead the team to victory.

Coaches must assess all the relevant characteristics of their team (as shown in figure 8.1), but pitching must be evaluated first because the rest of the team philosophy (defense and offense) will be influenced by the answers to the pitching assessment. For example, if a team doesn't have strong pitching, the coach knows that the team will be in high-scoring games; therefore, the team must develop an offense that will score a lot of runs. Pitching strengths or weaknesses have a lot of influence on how the coach will structure the team's offense to win games. So, the coach should examine the team's pitching and should answer the following questions:

- Does the team have an outstanding pitching staff that will keep the opponent from scoring many runs? Or is pitching a weakness that will allow opponents to score on the team frequently?
- Will the pitchers strike out a lot of batters or will they need to rely on the defense behind them in order to make outs?
- Are the pitchers down-ball pitchers who will induce ground-ball outs? Or are they rise-ball pitchers who will get batters to pop up more?
- Do the pitchers have good control or will they give up a lot of walks and thus put extra pressure on the defense?
- How well does the pitching staff handle the pressure of a close game in which every pitch matters?

The answers to these questions will influence the team's offensive strategy. If the team has great pitching that won't give up too many runs, the team may only need to score one or two runs per game in order to win. If the pitching staff is going to struggle to keep the score low, the team may have to score several runs per game in order to achieve a victory. The team's offensive strategy will be different depending on the strength of the team's pitching staff.

Next, the coach should evaluate the team's defense. Most coaches believe that pitching and defense win championships. If a team has strong pitching and strong defensive players, the team won't need to score a lot to win. With strong pitching, the coach should place the team's best defensive players in positions where more balls are likely to be put in play. If the pitcher tends to get a lot of ground balls to the left side, the team's best skilled defenders should be at shortstop and third base. If the pitcher throws a lot of drop balls, the coach must be sure to develop a catcher who can block the balls in the dirt. These are just a couple of examples of the type of defensive evaluations that coaches need to make in order to give their team the best chance of success.

If pitching is the weakest part of the team, the coach should sacrifice defense in order to get the team's strongest offensive threats on the field. No matter how good a defensive player is, she can't defend the walk or the home run. And line drives blasted all over the field are pretty tough too! With weak pitching, a team will likely be in a lot of slugfests and will need to score several runs to win. The coach should use the nine spots in the lineup to maximize the batting order and build a team based on offense. Also, the coach should build confidence in the players and encourage them to believe that they can always score more than the opponent no matter how many runs the opponent scores.

CHOOSE AN OFFENSIVE PLAN

After evaluating the team's pitching and defense, the coach will be ready to formulate the team's offensive strategy. How many runs will it take for the team to win games? The answer to this question will dictate the offensive strategy. If the team only needs one or two runs per game, the team will be able to play a little more conservatively on offense. If the team must generate six to eight runs per game in order to win, the offense will likely need to be more aggressive.

Once the coach has determined what the team needs to produce offensively to win, the next step is looking at what skills the team's players possess and how those skills will best contribute to the offensive strategy. Does the team have better power hitters or speed players? Can power and speed be combined into the game plan? The answers to these types of questions will determine the team's offensive strategy.

Even teams with solid power hitters in the lineup should develop the ability to play small ball. When a team can play small ball, the players will be confident that they can push across a run or two when needed. At some point, the team is likely to face an opponent with strong pitching and defense. The team needs to have other options besides waiting for the three-run home run, which may not come off of a great pitcher. As stated previously, it's good to have a lot of tools in your toolbox. Small-ball skills include the following:

- Having the ability to sacrifice bunt
- Being a patient hitter who is disciplined at the plate and can draw a walk
- Being able to put the ball in play on the ground when necessary to move a runner
- Having the ability to execute the hit-and-run
- Having the ability to execute the suicide squeeze
- Having base-stealing speed and smarts

Note that all of the previous skills can be perfected by right-handed batters. And if the team also has left-handed slappers, the weapons for playing small ball expand greatly. The slap-and-run and the contact play are great tools that slappers can use to move runners and score runs.

Of course, a coach shouldn't turn all power hitters into bunters just because the team has the pitching and defense to keep them in games. If a team can win games 7-0 with home runs and doubles in the gap, the team should go for it. However, a coach should prepare the team for the inevitable situation where the pitching is equal and the team's power hitters are struggling. The team needs to have another strategy for close, low-scoring games.

If the team's pitching is average at best, the offense will need to be the most high-powered piece of the team, and the majority of practice time should be spent working on offense. This team should throw conservative out the window and do whatever it takes to generate as many runs as possible. Whether the team's strength is speed or power, the coach can build an explosive offense. Power can generally get results a little quicker because one swing of the bat from a power hitter can produce a game-changing home run. Slappers tend to move runners one base at a time, so the team will need to string together more hits, defensive errors, and so on, in order to produce runs. Base stealing becomes very important—a speedy slapper can reach base on an error and can be at third via two stolen bases before the next batter has even completed her at-bat. If speed is the team's best asset, the coach must understand that the players may run themselves out of a few innings by being aggressive. There is always a chance that players will get thrown out stealing bases or trying to take the extra base on a hit. This aggressive type of philosophy relies on the defense making mistakes. Sometimes the defense will execute well and shut down a risky attempt on offense. But a team that relies on offense and is built around speed will have to take risks in order to achieve rewards.

Very few teams are great in every phase of the game. Great coaches identify the team's abilities and then design a game plan to play within those abilities. This process must occur each new season (and sometimes at midseason if injuries significantly affect the team). Great coaches also convince their players to embrace and take pride in the team's strengths and to build an identity around those strengths. Coaches can even play a "game within a game" and keep their own score by tracking how often their players execute the skills that form and support the team's identity. The players will gain a lot of confidence from seeing success in the process regardless of the outcome on the scoreboard.

CHAPTER 9

Communication

oftball has been called an individual game within a team concept. In basketball, a player's teammates can help set her up for a good shot by setting a pick. In volleyball, the hitter relies on a good pass from her teammate in order to spike the ball successfully. Although softball is a team sport, when a batter is in the box facing a pitcher, it's a one-on-one duel. Teammates and coaches can't do much to help other than provide encouragement. Despite the individual aspects of softball, communication between coaches and players and among players is critical to a successful offense. Important information should be communicated during a pregame scouting report. In addition, communication should take place when players are in the dugout waiting for at-bats, when they are in the on-deck circle, when they are in the batter's box during an at-bat, and when they are on the bases. This communication is essential for the team to work together and properly execute offensive plays that lead to scoring runs.

PREGAME SCOUTING REPORT

When possible, coaches should scout their opponent and provide information to their team. When preparing the offense to face another team, coaches should learn specific information about the opponent's players at each position. Figure 9.1 provides a list of the information that coaches should try to obtain for the pregame scouting report.

A coach's pregame scouting tasks should also include gathering information about the field conditions. Is the field hard or soft? This is important for the team's slappers to know. Is the field wet? If so, base runners should be more aggressive in taking extra bases, knowing that the outfielders will be handling a wet ball. How much distance is there from home plate to the backstop? This will dictate whether base runners on third base can score on a passed ball or wild pitch. How big is the foul territory? If it's extensive, runners may have an opportunity to tag and advance on a caught foul ball. How does the ball bounce off the backstop and off the outfield fence? This information will influence decisions made by base coaches and base runners.

These are just some examples of the types of things that coaches should consider telling their team about the upcoming game. By no means will a coach share all of the listed information. With a pregame scouting report, a coach must be sure not to give the players too much information. The coach must also gauge which players need more or less information. Some players like a lot of information, and it helps them play with more confidence. Others will suffer from "information overload" and will think too much rather than play on instinct. Ultimately, players should be focused on their own performance and not the opponent. However, information can be advantageous if players use it to help them execute in a given situation. Typically, coaches look for a weakness that the team can exploit, and they make sure the players are aware of it. For example, an opposing pitcher may not be able to throw overhand

Figure 9.1 Pregame Scouting Form

Position and player characteristics	Notes
PITCHER	
Speed	
Control	
Anything unique about her motion and delivery	
Go-to pitch—What does she throw when she needs a strike?	
Strikeout pitch—What does she throw when ahead in the count?	
Ability to change speeds—How often does she change speeds? Can she throw the changeup for a strike?	
Does she throw down a lot? (This can make it easier to steal bases.)	
Can players or coaches read the ball down or the changeup early out of her hand?	
Tendencies in various counts	
Fielding and throwing ability	
CATCHER	
Arm strength	
Release time—How quickly does she get rid of the ball on a steal?	
Arm accuracy	
Quickness	
Blocking ability	
Fielding ability	
Does she like to attempt pickoffs?	
CORNER PLAYERS	
Quickness	
Fielding and throwing ability	
Ability to play the bunt	
Ability to cover the 5-6 and 3-4 holes	
How well do they defend the slap?	
How well do they cover bases on the steal?	
MIDDLE INFIELDERS	
Range	
Fielding and throwing ability	
Positioning for slappers—What will they give up (soft or hard slap)?	
How well do they cover bases on the steal?	
OUTFIELDERS	
Arm strength	
Arm accuracy	
Range	
Positioning for slappers—Do they play shallow or deep?	

From R. Weekly and K. Weekly, 2012, *High-scoring softball* (Champaign, IL: Human Kinetics).

well. In this case, coaches would tell their slappers to drag bunt to the pitcher and would have their right-handed hitters do the same in bunt situations. If the catcher is slow getting rid of the ball on steals, coaches may put runners in motion more often than they normally would.

Coaches may also talk to their team about how the opponent plays under pressure. A shortstop or outfielder may have a great arm and look fantastic during pregame warm-up, but this same player may have a tendency to throw the ball away in a pressure situation. Coaches may want their runners to know that they should challenge this player to make a play under pressure anytime they can.

IN THE DUGOUT

During the game, coaches and players should look for things that may be different from the scouting report or new information that was unavailable before the game. If a team has never seen the opponents or did not receive a scouting report on them, all of the information that would have been contained in the pregame scouting report must be communicated in the dugout as the game unfolds. Hitting is a game of adjustment, and a team must constantly look for adjustments they can make during a game to help their offensive players be more successful.

From the dugout, hitters should watch for tendencies and patterns in the sequence of pitches so that they can answer the following questions:

- Is the pitcher throwing first-pitch strikes? How often? What type of pitch?
- What does she throw when ahead in the count?
- What does she throw when behind in the count?
- What does she throw in a bunt situation?
- Does she struggle to throw strikes?

A lot of communication should take place in the dugout among coaches and players about the things they are seeing from the pitcher. Batters who hit at the top of the order should immediately relay information about their at-bat to the rest of the team when they return to the dugout. Typically, two coaches are on the field coaching bases, and a third coach is in the dugout. One of the primary jobs of the coach in the dugout is to look for pitching and defensive tendencies and to communicate those to the team. That coach also makes sure that teammates are communicating with one another and continually looking for adjustments that can be made in order to improve the team's chances of scoring.

Slappers should look for defensive positioning as well as pitching tendencies and should communicate this information with each other in the dugout. The defense always gives them something, whether it is an opening to bunt, soft slap, or hard slap. A good slapper will recognize the weakness and exploit it. If the corners play back, the slapper has an opportunity to drag bunt. If the corners play in, this opens up the hard slap. If the shortstop plays deep, a soft slap will likely be successful. If the outfield plays shallow, slappers can try to drive the ball over them or through the gaps. Slappers also need to make note of who is covering bases on steals. Knowing whether the shortstop or second-base player covers second with a slapper at the plate and a runner on first is very important for the slapper in deciding what her best option is. The slappers should be constantly communicating with one another about what they are seeing and what tool they think will work the best.

IN THE ON-DECK CIRCLE

As the hitter moves to the on-deck circle, she should be getting her mind relaxed and ready to hit. Coaches don't need to provide too much information at this point. Yogi Berra once said, "How can I think and hit at the same time?" A coach may remind the hitter of her pregame plan or alert a slapper to a shift in defensive positioning, but the coach definitely doesn't want to flood the hitter with a lot of instructions. It's time for the player's natural instincts and talents to take over. A relaxed mind and body are able to perform at an optimal level.

The on-deck batter does have responsibility for communicating with a runner coming home. She is like a base coach at home plate. As soon as the ball is put in play, the on-deck batter must get in position behind home plate and must face third base (making sure she isn't so close that she interferes with the play; see figure 9.2); she instructs the base runner on whether to slide and where to slide. This is a very important piece of communication and must be practiced. On-deck batters tend to get caught up in the excitement of the action and forget to move into position. Failure to communicate at home plate can be the difference in scoring or not scoring a run and ultimately in winning or losing a game.

Figure 9.2   On-deck batter coaching the base runner.

DURING AN AT-BAT

Essential communication occurs between the coach and players during an at-bat, especially when runners are on base. The coach typically communicates with batters and base runners via a signal system that allows the coach to instruct the players without calling time-outs for conferences (the rules limit the number of conferences allowed). Although signals are commonly relayed from the coach at third base, signals may also be given from first base or the dugout. The number of signs and the method of relaying them to the players are a matter of personal preference. Coaches need to have a signal for every play they want their offense to execute. Common plays that a team will need signals for include the following:

- Bunt
- Steal
- Hit-and-run
- Bunt-and-run
- Suicide squeeze
- Fake bunt
- Take the pitch
- Contact play

If the team has slappers in the lineup, the coach may also want to include signs for various types of slaps (soft, hard, chop) and for the slap-and-run play. The coach should keep it simple so that the players can understand and remember the signs. The last thing a coach wants is for the players to be stepping into the box worried about whether they know the signs. This is a time when they need to be relaxed. The team should spend practice time on giving and receiving signals so that the players are comfortable and confident in their ability to understand the signs.

Coaches have many signal systems to choose from. The key is that the coach and players are comfortable with the system and are communicating effectively. Coaches traditionally use a hand-and-body signal system that involves touching various parts of the body or clothing. Here are three hand-and-body signal methods:

- **Indicator method.** The coach designates an indicator, and the next touch after the indicator relays the instruction. Let's assume that the indicator is the nose. The coach may have four signs and may use body parts to communicate them as follows: ear (bunt), hat or visor (steal), hand (hit-and-run), shoulder (squeeze). The body part or clothing touched after the nose is the sign or instruction. The coach may go through a series of touches, but the players are only looking for the coach to touch his nose and the sign immediately following that.

- **Number of touches.** The coach designates an indicator that opens and closes the sign. The number of touches between the open and close determines the signal and the play called. Let's assume that the indicator is the nose again, and that the coach has the same four signs as mentioned previously. Now each sign has a number attached to it—for example, 1 is bunt, 2 is steal, 3 is hit-and-run, and 4 is squeeze. The players look for the indicator (nose) and then count the number of touches to any body or clothing part until the coach touches the indicator (nose) again. The number represents the play that the coach wants executed. For instance, the coach may touch her nose, followed by a touch to the ear, then the hat, then the hand, and then back to the nose. In this case, the play called is the hit-and-run because there were three touches between the touches to the nose.
- **Place in coach's box.** In this method, the coach touches various body and clothing parts, but all of the touches are meaningless. The sign is determined by where the coach is standing in the coach's box. For example, the sideline could signal steal, the back could signal bunt, the middle could signal hit-and-run, and the front line could signal squeeze.

More teams have recently started using a numbers system. Each player wears a wristband with a clear sleeve holder for holding a card. The card contains a list of numbers, and each number correlates to a play. For example, steal could be associated with 10 to 15 random numbers on a given day, such as 121, 156, 183, 240, 255, 297, and so on (the same would be done for any other signs the team uses). The coach has a card with the same numbers. The coach simply calls out the number, and the players check their wristbands to see which play is called. For each game, new numbers are assigned to the various signals, and the players are given the new card to place in their wristband.

ON THE BASES

In addition to the signs that the coach uses to simultaneously communicate plays to both the batter and base runners, the coach will need to communicate in other ways with just the base runners. This communication can be verbal or nonverbal depending on the situation.

At times, the coach may want to put the steal on but not alert the batter. In this situation, the coach will give a sign to the base runner after the batter has stepped into the batter's box. This may also catch the defense unaware because they won't see the coach going through the series of signs. If the coach sees an opportunity for a delayed steal (a runner advancing a base when the catcher throws the ball back to the pitcher), the coach will need a sign to alert the base runner.

After the ball is put into play, coaches must communicate with base runners regarding whether they want them to advance a base or stop. A team should have nonverbal signals for communicating in these situations because crowd noise, cheering from the teams on the field, and defensive play calling can drown out the coach's verbal communication to the player.

We teach our base runners to make decisions on their own as much as possible when running the bases. Whenever they can see the play develop, we want them to trust their eyes and make the decision about whether to stop or advance. This forces them to keep their head up and keep their eyes on the play at all times. Runners will make quicker decisions with their eyes than when they look away from the play to find the base coach and then process information that the base coach is relaying with hand signals and voice commands. For example, a runner on first can see the base hit that lands anywhere from the left-field line to right center, and she can see the fielders react to the ball. She can make a quick read about whether or not she can advance to third base or must stop at second. When she trusts her eyes, she will likely be able to make the decision to advance to third without ever breaking her momentum.

In practices, we allow our players to make their own decisions on the bases almost all of the time. We encourage them to err on the side of being overly aggressive yet smart. They learn how to read ball speed and angle off the bat, how to read defensive players, and how to read outfield angles. They also learn to test their limits. There may be times in the game when the coach does not want to leave the decision in the base runner's hands. The coach may want the runners to be extra aggressive early in the game but may want them to defer to the coach more in the late innings. The coach must make sure that the players understand when they are on their own and when they need to look to the coach.

When the runner can't see the ball or the defensive play being made, the runner must rely on the base coaches. Good communication is essential in these situations. First, the coach must get in a good position in the coach's box so that the runner can clearly see the signals being given. The coach may have to move within the box as the play develops in order for the runner to maintain a good visual line with the coach. The coach's signals must be clear and understandable. In practice, the team should go over what hand motions the coach will use to communicate various instructions.

The first-base coach needs to do one of three things when a batter–runner puts the ball in play:

- If the ball is hit to the infield and the runner is running through first base, the coach should do nothing.
- If the runner will safely reach first base but will likely not be able to advance to second, the coach should motion for the runner to turn and look (the coach wants the runner to round first and find the ball; see figure 9.3).
- If the runner will likely be able to make it to second base, the coach should motion to the runner to round first base and continue to second (see figure 9.4). After the runner passes first base, any necessary instructions will be given by the third-base coach.

Figure 9.3   Coach signals runner to turn and look.

Figure 9.4   Coach signals runner to continue to second base.

Figure 9.5   Runner looking for third-base coach when the play is behind her.

Figure 9.6   Third-base coach motioning runner to slide.

If the ball is behind the runner and she cannot see the play (a ball hit down the right-field line), she must pick up the third-base coach when she is halfway to second base (see figure 9.5). The third-base coach now motions for the runner to continue past second and advance to third or to stop at second base. If the coach motions for the runner to advance and a play is being made on the runner coming into third base, the coach must direct the runner whether to stand or slide (see figure 9.6). If the runner will slide, the coach should also indicate which side of the base to slide to. Most coaches do this by motioning with their hands down toward the ground to one side or the other.

When a runner begins the play on second base and the batter gets a base hit to the outfield, the runner will rely on the third-base coach's instruction to determine whether to stop at third or advance home (see figure 9.7 and 9.8). The coach may not be able to make the decision before the runner reaches third base. In that case, the coach will likely have to wave the runner around third; then, if the coach decides not to send the runner home, the coach will put up the stop sign in time for the runner to put on the brakes and return to third base. The coach will need to move down the line toward home as the play is developing (see figure 9.9) so that the runner can see when the coach's signal changes.

Another play that requires good communication is the tag-up play. When runners begin the play on first or third base and a potential tag-up play arises, the base coach is close enough to use verbal commands with the runner. When the ball is in the air, the coach will instruct the runner to tag up. Some coaches don't want the runner to watch the ball; instead, they want the runner to listen for the coach to say "go" when the ball is caught. Other coaches like the runner

Figure 9.7   Third-base coach signaling runner to advance.

Figure 9.8   Third-base coach signaling runner to stop.

Figure 9.9   Third-base coach signaling after runner has rounded third base.

to watch the catch and to use her eyes to time her departure. Coaches who prefer the latter method will need to tell the runner "yes" or "no" while the ball is in the air so that she knows whether the coach wants her to advance on the catch or remain at the base. The only decision that the coach is leaving in the runner's hands is when to leave the base. When the runner begins the play on second base and the coach wants her to tag and advance, the coach will tell her "tag," and the runner will watch the catch to time her departure. If the runner hears nothing, she trusts her eyes and reacts to the play as it develops.

Sometimes there is simply not enough time for the coach to issue a command and for the player to process and react to that command. By the time all of that happens, the opportunity is lost. Therefore, communication before the play is essential. A great example of this situation is when a runner on third base must determine whether she should try to score on a wild pitch or passed ball. The player's speed, the distance from home to the backstop, how the ball bounces off the backstop, and other factors will play a role in this decision. Pregame information relayed in the scouting report is critical here. The coach should also talk to the player when she reaches third base about what to look for and whether the coach wants her to be aggressive at that point in the game. Then it is up to the player to react quickly and get a good jump once she sees the ball get past the catcher.

Another example is when a runner on third must decide whether to try to score on an infield ground ball. Before the pitch, the coach should communicate with the runner about where the infielders are playing and whether the coach thinks the runner has a chance to score on a ball hit to a particular infielder. With that information in her data bank, the runner is again responsible for making her read and decision quickly. If a team's players know the coach's philosophy (whether the coach wants them to be aggressive in a given situation) and if the coach is consistent with that philosophy, the runners will more often than not make decisions that the coach agrees with. Remember, if the coach likes the players to run the bases aggressively, they will make some outs while doing so. The coach must let the runners know that it's okay to make mistakes when being aggressive. As the season progresses, the runners will get better at making the right decisions.

CHAPTER **10**

The Mental Game

ractice builds confidence, and confidence builds success. These words are often said when coaches discuss hitting. Confidence is only one portion of the mental game, but it is the most important aspect of being a successful hitter. In this chapter, we discuss the mental challenges facing hitters and provide some strategies—both physical and mental—that will help batters succeed when they step into the batter's box.

The first mental concept that players need to understand is the GIGO principle. Simply said, GIGO means "garbage in, garbage out," or the positive translation of "good in, good out." Early in our college coaching career, we had an outstanding but inconsistent hitter who told us the following: "When I get in the batter's box, I feel like I have a separate voice in each ear. The voice in my right ear tells me how good I am, and the voice in my left ear tells me I am terrible." Players must understand that they are what they think they are—and that a player will do what her mind tells her to do. Many young players fear failure. This fear of failure is the main reason why many players are unsuccessful in hitting and other softball skills. These players fear failure because they are not prepared mentally and physically to play the game. The bigger the challenge, the higher the fear factor. Coaches at all levels must prepare their players mentally as well as physically.

Based on our experience—which has included coaching and observing all levels from youth baseball to Olympic softball, researching numerous publications on the mental game, and interacting with top coaches at both the national and international level—we have learned that the following strategies are consistent with success:

- Locking on with your team to create an inner circle of focus
- Remembering the 20-80 rule
- Developing a mental game plan
- Sticking with the process
- Becoming a clutch player
- Using positive self-talk
- Using visualization
- Making mental adjustments between pitches
- Performing self-evaluation

These strategies are not new, and we can't take credit for creating them. However, we have implemented these strategies with our team, and we believe they are directly responsible for our team's four top-three finishes in the Women's College World Series. At Tennessee, we distribute a mental game notebook to each player. The mental game notebook is a collection of handouts and articles on various topics related to mental preparation. Examples of these topics include focus, visualization, positive energy, self-talk, enthusiasm, attitude, and a champion's mind-set. Some of the handouts have been staples of our program for years. Others are items that we have found more recently and implemented into the notebook. We are constantly looking for stories and articles that communicate an important aspect of the mental game.

We have meetings once a week to discuss the mental game, and we design mental strategies for each opponent. We believe strongly in preparing the mind to compete. Each player assesses her mental game skills; then we go over the assessment with the player to discuss strengths and weaknesses, as well as ways to improve in various areas. Each player will also prepare a mental game plan. For example, the player will write a plan for her at-bats. This plan will include the thoughts and self-talk that the player will use in the dugout, in the on-deck circle, and in the batter's box. A pitcher will prepare a similar plan for her thought processes and approach in between pitches on the field, as well as in the dugout between innings.

LOCKING ON

Most players are bombarded with outside influences, and they struggle with trying to live up to everyone's expectations. These outside factors can severely hamper the players' chances for success. In most cases, players are trying to please everyone but themselves. These outside distractions are even more common at higher levels. At the Olympic Games in Atlanta in 1996, we had to shield our players from all outside influences because the demands on them were so high. Family members wanting tickets, media wanting interviews, and friends wanting to visit the Olympic Village were just a few of the distractions that threatened the players' rest and ultimately their performance. These distractions limited the players' focus on the real challenge—the gold medal. At younger levels, youth and high school players are always trying to live up to expectations from family, friends, and media. Coaches need to recognize when players are mentally tired, stressed, and in need of reassurance.

On arrival at the competition site, we use a strategy that we refer to as "lock on." This strategy involves creating a secure inner circle of only the players and coaches. During lock-on time, players keep their focus within this inner circle and avoid contact with those outside the circle. This enables the players to relax, go over their pregame plan, and focus on the challenges they will face in the game. Players leave their baggage at the gate, and they lock on when they enter the locker room or when they enter the playing field to begin pregame warm-up. The outer circle consists of family, friends, umpires, media, and fans. At the college level, we ask the parents to enjoy the game as fans and to leave the coaching to us. The parents know that they will have no contact with the players from the beginning of lock-on time until after our postgame meeting and the players' subsequent release. This strategy is very effective in freeing up the players to simply play the game. Coaches must be sure to educate the players' parents about the reason for this policy and how it helps the players perform at a higher level.

REMEMBERING THE 20-80 RULE

This is a strategy for everyday life as well as for softball. It expresses the idea that most people spend too much time worrying about why something happened rather than what they are going to do about it. Thus, the 20-80 rule states that life is 20 percent what happens to you and 80 percent how you react to it. When we took the U.S. team to a third-world country in 1995 for the Pan American qualifier, some of the other teams spent the whole time worrying about the quality of the lodging, the food, the stadium, and so on. We reminded our players of the 20-80 rule, and they embraced it. We made the best of the situation and actually had a good time competing and being together. We used the inner circle (or lock on) strategy in addition to the 20-80 rule. We went undefeated, were not scored on, and won the gold medal. Many of our opponents spent the entire time complaining. They were more focused on the less-than-desirable living conditions and food choices than they were on the games, and it showed in their performance. The members of the U.S. team who made that trip now look back on it as one of the most fun experiences they had playing softball. The team's attitude could be summed up with this saying: "If life gives you lemons, make lemonade."

At Tennessee, we talk about the 20-80 rule a lot. We want our players to accept that everything will not always go their way. Worrying about the previous play often causes players to fail. Softball is a game of inches. A player may get a bad call, get a bad break, or simply have something go wrong. When these things occur, the player must pick herself up, dust herself off, and go again. The best players in the game think only of the next pitch or the next play. Everything that has happened in the past is over forever. Players must concentrate on the future!

Another common saying related to the mental game is "flush it." Flush it means to simply get rid of a thought or action by mentally flushing it down the drain. Sport psychologists often advise players to use this method to help alleviate a bad play or negative thought. If a player flushes a bad pitch or bad swing, she is clearing her mind for the next pitch. This is similar to the 20-80 rule, because it symbolically eliminates the bad play or bad thought from the player's mind.

DEVELOPING A MENTAL GAME PLAN

Planning is important in any task that a person undertakes. Every softball player needs a practice plan. Every softball player also needs a mental game plan. The mental game plan helps ensure that the player is mentally prepared to face any situation she may encounter in the upcoming game. The player should start creating this plan early in the week when she is evaluating the upcoming opponent. The player should think about past contests with the team and pitcher. What pitches have they thrown her in the past? How has the defense played her? What can she expect based on what has occurred in the past? If game video exists, she should watch it. If not, she should discuss the previous games with the coach. If the opponent's past strategy was not effective against the player, she should think about what the opponent might do to be more successful this time. This information should be the foundation of the player's mental game plan. The player's practice time should then be geared toward countering any adversity she faced in the last game and helping her build confidence that she can be more successful this time. Confidence can never be overrated. If certain opponent strategies caused problems for the player in a previous game, she should work on adjustments and repetitions in practice. This can give her confidence that she can beat the strategy. Physical preparation improves a player's mental approach, because it helps the player believe that she is ready to counter the opponent's strategy.

Developing a mental game plan may also include studying a handout on focus or visualization. In addition, each player should write a short goal sheet as part of the mental game plan. The goal sheet reminds the player of what type of mind-set she wants to have when she arrives at the ball field, and it specifies what she wants her thoughts to be during warm-up, in the dugout, in the on-deck circle, and in the batter's box. These goals are all designed to help the player think positive. Players can write their goals on a wristband, a 3-by-5-inch card, a visor lining, or even the inside of their glove. Softball players commonly use abbreviations and acronyms. We had a very good pitcher who wanted to glorify God when she played. She would always write LGLG on her wristband or visor to remind her to "let go, let God." This was a form of release for her when things were not going correctly. We had another player who used the acronym MAGIC, standing for "make a greater individual commitment." Regardless of a player's personal beliefs, her plan should include a coping mechanism that reminds her that she is mentally strong and can overcome adversity when it strikes. For many players, this involves visualizing a "happy place" during adversity—for example, they may visualize their favorite place to relax. They simply take a deep breath, close their eyes, and think of this favorite spot.

Regardless of which coping mechanism a player uses, she must be sure to have one as part of her plan. In the movie *For Love of the Game,* Kevin Costner's character was able to completely block out the fans, the opponent, and the noise—everything but the catcher's glove—by repeating the words *Clear the mechanism.* The mind is an extremely important part of a player's game preparation. If a player believes it, she can achieve it. Remember, failing to plan means planning to fail.

STICKING WITH THE PROCESS

The process refers to what a player does physically and mentally to prepare to play. The process would include the player's physical plan, her mental plan, and the strategies she intends to use to achieve victory on the playing field. Sticking with the process is important. Many players spend an entire week (or even an entire preseason) developing a certain way to respond both mentally and physically, and then at the first hint of adversity, they abandon the process. When a player abandons the process, she leaves herself and her team in a no-man's-land with little or no chance of success.

Players with a strong mental game realize that adversity will occur in any contest. The best-laid plans can unravel temporarily, but character is born in adversity. Sticking to the game plan, or staying with the process, means that players should continue to do what they do best and not give in to the opponent's game plan. One key phrase in coaching is "play your own best self," which means stick to the process. Players cannot control what their opponent does, but they can control their reaction to it. This goes back to the 20-80 rule. Remember, the process is designed to accentuate the things that the player and her team do best. The process is designed to give the player the best chance for success in all phases of the game. A strong mental player believes in her coaches, her teammates, and the game plan. A strong mental player believes in the process.

BECOMING A CLUTCH PLAYER

Every player wants to be known as a clutch player—that is, the type of player that the coach wants in the batter's box or on the mound with the game on the line. Clutch players *want* that pressure, and their performance almost always equals their potential. The clutch player has a very strong mental game and enjoys being the one in the spotlight with the game or championship on the line.

We ask our players to watch the movie *Hoosiers,* starring Gene Hackman. In the movie, the star athlete—named Jimmy Chitwood—asks for the ball and the last shot in a state championship game. He gets the ball, makes the shot, and wins the championship for his team and his school. We want our players to be like Jimmy Chitwood. With this in mind, we award a "JC" helmet sticker to the outstanding clutch player in each game we play. To become a clutch player, an athlete must work long and hard to perfect her skills. This enables her to believe in her ability to make the big play. Clutch players have a strong mental game plan, and they do not focus on the possibility of failure. These players rarely think negative thoughts, and when they catch themselves doing so, they have a strategy in place to change to a more positive mind-set. They consistently play at a high level mentally and physically. No one is perfect, and no one bats 1.000. Clutch players understand this and have strategies to deal with the pressure and the fear of failure that can consume other players who are less successful.

Clutch players have a strong inner game. They play each play as if it could decide the game. They keep in mind that they never know when the opportunity will come that will decide the game; therefore, they never take a play off. In the fall, we have our players play a series of games that we call crazy Olympics. I learned these games and the reason for using them from one of the best coaches I ever knew. His philosophy was to get players to compete in any game, even games not related to softball. This may include blind football, shuttle races, wheelbarrow races, or any of several other crazy games. Competition in games is the best way to identify a clutch player. Clutch players approach every contest with an eager mind-set; they are determined to win and determined to be the one who enables their team to win. You can see it in their eyes. They were born to compete.

USING POSITIVE SELF-TALK

Positive self-talk is a simple but very effective skill for enhancing the mental game. Remember the children's book titled *The Little Engine That Could*? The engine kept saying to itself, "I think I can, I think I can." With this positive mind-set, the little engine overcame every obstacle. The GIGO principle— "good in, good out" versus "garbage in, garbage out"—was discussed earlier in the chapter. This is a principle that coaches must teach and stress at every level. It should be a normal part of a team's practice. Players should be taught to always use "put-ups," not put-downs. Coaches and staff should always instruct in a positive manner, not a negative manner.

Here is an example of keeping a coaching point positive: "Keep the bat above the ball and get the bunt down." This is better than stating the point in a negative way: "Do not pop up the bunt." If a coach uses negative statements when teaching, or if the players communicate to each other in a negative manner, this could become a self-fulfilling prophecy and lead to a player executing the wrong way instead of the right way. When coaching a U.S. team in the late 1990s, we developed the acronym FIST, which stood for "focus, intensity, strong together." If a player made an error or failed to execute a play properly, the player would tap her chest to indicate that she knew how to do it right. The coaching staff and other players would look at this player and give her a thumbs-up in order to send her this message: "That's OK, we are with you."

The real key here is that the players must truly believe they are prepared to play. They must be confident and positive in every endeavor. Confidence is earned through practice and preparation. We continually tell our players that success in any skill they undertake—whether it is playing golf, playing a musical instrument, or riding a horse—requires three things: confidence, discipline, and repetition. Those three factors will ensure success. The person must know how to do it, must be confident that she can do it, and must do it over and over. If she believes it, she will achieve it. If a player believes in her skills, her inner voice will be very positive, and her performance will also be positive.

USING VISUALIZATION

Visualization, imagery, and relaxation techniques are very important aspects of the mental game. These strategies deal with the mind's eye, and if practiced correctly, they can definitely improve the physical part of a player's game. One study involving NBA players had a group shooting 25 free throws a day for one week. A second group never took an actual shot, but these players visualized shooting 25 free throws a day for the same period. At the conclusion of this study, both groups competed in a free-throw contest. The group that visualized and did not shoot had basically the same shooting percentage as the group that actually shot free throws each day. The mind is a person's most powerful tool. Great athletes train their minds as well as their bodies.

The best way for a player to visualize is to find a quiet spot and totally relax her body for 10 to 15 minutes. This is best done when the player is lying flat on her back, with her palms extended up. Once comfortable, the player closes her eyes and takes several deep breaths. Then she tenses and relaxes each muscle in her body. She starts with her feet and then moves to her legs, hips, back, shoulders, arms, hands, and face. She tenses these muscles for approximately 5 seconds each. At the conclusion, she takes three more deep breaths. The player should feel her body relax and should spend a few minutes enjoying that relaxed state. This is the formal relaxation technique that athletes have been taught for years, and it is still very popular today. In times past, coaches would have an entire football team lie on their backs in a darkened gymnasium and go through the relaxation technique before visualizing an upcoming game. Within minutes, half the team was so relaxed that they had to fight off sleep.

Today's athletes like this technique, but being from the "I want it now generation," they would prefer to relax a little quicker. Their pre-visualization technique is done sitting up and includes their iPod and headset. They claim that they can block out everything and visualize in this manner. This is a better technique than no technique at all, but psychologists indicate that visualization is more effective with the old method of relaxing. The iPod and music could be used in either method.

Once the player is relaxed, the process of visualization begins. The player starts by seeing herself on the field where her game will be played; she sees this through her own eyes, not watching herself from a spectator's point of view. She should see it in first person and in color, and she should use all her senses. She controls this session. She should feel as many sensations as she can. She can even try to smell the dirt, feel the wind, and hear the crowd. The more realistic the imagery, the better the player's mind's eye will record the session. The player should visualize four specific situations four times each. These should be situations that the player anticipates will occur in the game (possibly situations that she has struggled with in the past). The player must see the situations clearly and in this sequence:

1. The player sees the situation at normal speed, sharpening her image of the play.
2. The player sees the situation over again in slow motion, from start to finish.
3. The player sees the play in a clutch situation at normal speed (she should really get into the play).
4. The player sees the situation one more time at normal speed and actually feels herself executing the play.

Remember, there are no shortcuts. The visualization process just set forth is very different from merely thinking about your performance in an upcoming game. Players can use visualization techniques to improve their hitting skills and to help them master new techniques more quickly than through physical repetition alone.

- **Visualization technique as a learning tool.** When a coach wants to teach a new technique to an athlete, the visualization process will speed up the learning curve. Some very successful coaches build in time for imagery or visualization when teaching new skills to athletes. Imagery lets the athletes feel themselves doing a new technique before they actually do it. Athletes today are very visual learners. If they can combine imagery or visualization with actual physical repetition, they will reduce their learning time and become better performers because they will be training both the mind and the body. This is a very good technique for coaches to use when teaching hitting. Coaches can also use this teaching tool to reduce sloppiness and bad habits by having batters visualize perfect technique before stepping into the batter's box.

- **Visualization technique as applied directly to hitting.** When hitters talk about "being in the zone," they are referring to times when the ball seemed as big as a basketball and when the pitcher seemed to be putting the ball on a tee for them to hit. The hitter could do no wrong. Most players have experienced this at least once in their life, and every player would like to experience it as many times as possible. Some players have been fortunate enough to capture these moments on video. A player can also capture them in her mind's eye. To do so, the player remembers when hitting the ball seemed effortless. She visualizes that time or moment over and over, using the four-step process described earlier. She remembers her confident feeling as the ball struck the fat part of the bat.

Next, the player should think about the toughest pitchers in her league. What do they throw? What do they do that baffles the hitter? What does she expect when she faces them next? The player should get a good mental picture of this and then see herself facing that pitcher when in the zone. The player sees herself connecting solidly with the ball and encircling the bases. She sees and feels the admiration from her team, her coaches, and the fans. The player should enjoy the moment in her mind and replay it over and over. Finally, the player should visualize herself having that perfect practice. She feels very confident and sure of her ability. She steps into the box with a definite purpose that is clear in her mind. She sees herself hitting hard line drives in every gap and even putting a few shots over the fence.

- **If the mind can see it, the body can achieve it.** The only place where success comes ahead of work is in the dictionary. Relaxation, visualization, and imagery take time. The best athletes we have coached believed strongly in these techniques. The two Olympic gold-medal teams we worked with were trained in these techniques by highly qualified psychologists from the U.S. Olympic Committee. The teams embraced these techniques, used them, and became the best in the world.

MAKING MENTAL ADJUSTMENTS BETWEEN PITCHES

This section describes an excellent four-stage strategy that hitters can use during the 12- to 18-second cycle between every pitch. The time between pitches may vary by umpire and pitcher (and also because of recent rule changes designed to speed up the game). Regardless, each batter will always have several valuable seconds between every pitch in an at-bat. Players with a great mental game will use each distinctive stage between every pitch. These stages are also known as rituals. Watching softball players between pitches can be really fun. It is easy to tell which batters are ready for the next pitch and which ones are not ready. Failure to facilitate each stage, or pattern of activity, can result in a less successful at-bat. The four separate stages are as follows:

Stage 1: The Positive Response

The purpose of this stage is to facilitate the flow of positive thoughts and to reduce the chance that anger, disappointment, or any other disruptive response will interfere with the next pitch. This stage starts the second the previous pitch has ended and lasts for 2 or 3 seconds.

Physically, the batter should make a quick decisive movement with her body the instant the pitch is over. For example, if she did well, she could make a quick pumping action with her arm and fist. If she failed on the pitch, she can make a quick decisive move away from the mistake as if to indicate "no worries." She should pull her shoulders back, keeping her head up and her eyes forward. She wants to project high energy and a strong competitive image.

Mentally, the batter does not need to say anything to herself, but if she does, she should follow these guidelines: If she failed on the pitch, she should say "no problem" or "let it go." She can even praise her opponent by saying "nice job." This takes the pressure off herself. If she did well on the pitch, she can say "nice job" or "let's go."

Stage 2: The Relaxation Response

In this stage, the batter allows her body to recover from the physical and emotional stress of the previous pitch, and she returns her competitive level to an optimal range. This stage starts 2 or 3 seconds after the pitch occurs. The length of this stage is 4 to 6 seconds.

Physically, the batter continues the positive high-energy movement from stage 1. She moves around outside the batter's box. She can stretch, move the bat in her hands, or tighten the Velcro on her batting gloves. She should breathe deeply and slowly. The important thing here is that she keeps her feet moving. Under stressful conditions, blood will pool in the player's feet if she is not moving. Major-league players are always moving around between pitches. They all have a relaxation stage between pitches. The more stressful the previous pitch, or the more important the next pitch, the more time the batter needs in this stage.

Mentally, batters should think only relaxing, calming thoughts, such as *I'm OK, Settle down,* or *I know what to expect and I know how to handle it.*

Stage 3: The Preparation Response

The purpose of this stage is for the batter to ensure that she knows the situation and has thought about what she intends to do before the next pitch. This stage starts as soon as the batter begins to move into the ready position for the next pitch. The length of this stage is 3 or 4 seconds.

Physically, after achieving recovery in stage 2, the batter begins to move to the ready position by stepping toward the batter's box. She should look directly at the pitcher and project the strongest, most confident, and most aggressive image possible. She should project a powerful image that says to the pitcher, "I am confident that I will succeed."

Mentally, the batter needs to decide exactly what she wants to do with this pitch. In a sense, she is programming her mental computer and establishing a mind-set.

Stage 4: The Automatic Ritual Response

In this stage, the batter wants to achieve the highest state of mental and physical readiness before the pitcher delivers the pitch. This stage balances concentration and intensity with appropriate muscle relaxation, and it produces an instinctive, automatic state of anticipation. This stage starts as soon as the batter moves into the batter's box. The length of this stage is 3 to 5 seconds.

Physically, the batter should take a deep breath, allowing the shoulders to rise and lower and allowing the chest to expand and contract. A batter should develop and use some type of prepitch movement with the bat—for instance, bat circles or half swings.

Mentally, the batter should not think about technique and should not use any self-talk. She must simply focus on the pitcher, see the ball clearly, and hit the ball.

Initially, this four-stage routine will feel unnatural and forced, just like a new grip or swing technique. With practice, however, this routine will begin to feel like a normal part of the batter's prepitch routine. Every softball fan who watched the Olympic Games in 1996 remembers Dr. Dot Richardson's prepitch adjustments. She was dynamic with her movements just before stepping into the box.

An excellent way to practice the stages is to rehearse them in front of a mirror or on a field without an opponent. While mastering these stages, a player should make her performance between pitches just as important as her performance during play. Great players know that controlling their activity between pitches can be the extra edge needed to control their performance in the game.

PERFORMING SELF-EVALUATION

A final strategy for helping players develop a strong mental game is the use of a self-evaluation program that rates their performance in all offensive categories. We believe strongly in video analysis, and we require our players to watch their performances in both practice and actual competition. Feedback is the "breakfast of champions," and there is no better form of feedback than video analysis.

We design feedback sheets for each offensive skill and require the players to watch the film and then complete the forms. The coaches have already seen each player's performance firsthand and also on video. After receiving the player's self-evaluation, the coaches will then critique the player's evaluation and point out to her exactly what they expect the next day at practice. This is a very good system that creates written feedback between the coaches and players. The evaluation process is also an opportunity for coaches to point out things that the player did very well, in addition to things that the player needs to work on in practice.

Each player should complete a self-evaluation form for hitting, bunting, and baserunning. Each of these evaluations should contain a breakdown of specific skills within the category. Many examples of feedback sheets can be found. Players or coaches need to decide exactly what they want to evaluate and then prepare their forms accordingly. For example, at Tennessee, our evaluation forms for hitting include the player's name, the date, and the opponent. The forms also include the weather conditions and field conditions. We evaluate each at-bat, including the pitches thrown and what happened on each pitch. We also specify which pitches (both by spin and location) were more difficult for the batter to hit. We record RBIs, extra-base hits, and on-base percentage for that game. In addition, the forms include lots of room for comments by both the player and coach. When the player has completed her self-evaluation and the coaches have added their comments, we give a copy to the player and file a copy for future reference. This file is especially helpful when facing the same opponent in the future.

Appendix A: Offensive Circuit Training

As stated earlier in this book, hitting requires confidence, discipline, and repetition. The best way to get all three is through circuit training. We use some form of circuit training every day in our workouts. Circuit training is advantageous in many ways:

- Circuits can be designed to work on specific problem areas.
- Players get maximum repetitions in minimum time.
- Coaches get a lot of hands-on work with the players.
- Players get immediate and constant feedback on their performance.

DESIGNING A CIRCUIT

We are strong advocates of circuit training because it has been very valuable to our teams. In fact, we think that circuit training is the main reason we are successful as an offensive team. For younger players, coaches should keep the drills basic. Coaches should compile a list of drills that they like to use for each skill they are teaching. The coach must know the reason for each station and must be able to communicate the reason for the drill to the players. A team does not have to purchase expensive equipment for these drills. For teams that cannot afford all the new training devices, the Poor Man's Circuit in appendix B provides a circuit that does not require a high budget. The 150 Swings for Success in appendix C also provides a drill set that uses little equipment. In addition, the homemade equipment that coaches create is often just as good or better than the equipment on the market.

All coaches have many drills at their disposal. If a team has 20 players, the coach can divide them into teams of 2 and set up 10 stations. Two players are at each station. For this practice, let's say the coach wants to work on ensuring that players keep their hands high and do not drop or loop them during the swing. Further, the coach wants the players to keep their hands inside the ball and not cast or sweep. To work on this, the coach could set up a couple of standard stations—such as a standard tee and a front-toss station—and then set up 4 stations that focus on ensuring that players do not drop their hands during the swing. To help alleviate casting, the coach can set up 4 stations with drills that work on that challenge. An example would be the Wall Swing drill for slappers discussed in chapter 2 (see page 41). For nonslappers, the player measures her distance from the wall, net, or other barrier by placing the nub of the bat against her belly button and the head of the bat against a screen. The player must then swing without striking the screen (see figure 1). This teaches the batters to keep their hands inside the ball. A timekeeper helps keep the players moving through the

Figure 1   Proper setup near the net for nonslappers.

circuit. The hitters go from station 1 to station 2 and on through to station 10. Figure 2 provides a sample 10-station circuit.

We usually have 2 1/2 hours for practice, but most high school and summer teams have only 2 hours at the most. That is another reason to use circuit training for working on hitting. A team can use 1 hour for circuit training and the other hour for the remainder of practice. This will ensure that the team stays very strong offensively because each player can get 200 reps in the hour of circuit training.

Figure 3 on page 166 provides a sample practice plan for a 2 1/2-hour practice. Steps 1 and 2 deal with warm-ups, and steps 3 and 4 deal with defense. The defensive workouts, especially the special drills, should change daily based upon the team's needs. The defensive situational drills not only allow players to work on all the defensive skills but also allow players who are not in a defensive position to work on baserunning. Step 5 and the last hour of practice is devoted to hitting. If your team is limited to cages or indoor work, you might want to set up 10 stations like described in the sample circuit plan. If you have access to cages and a field for live hitting, you can split your team into two groups, one in the cages doing 5 stations and the other on the field hitting live. The team should use 5 circuit stations designed to practice the skills the team needs to work on and then the live hitting on the field session should focus on one or two specific skills. In this 2 1/2-hour practice plan, you can cover all facets of the game except pitching. The pitchers will work on their own with the pitching coach. During the hour of hitting, each player should get a minimum of 250 cuts. The practice plan for each day of practice should focus on what the coach perceives to be the most pressing issues with the team. If a team needs additional hitting, bunting, or slapping practice, more of the 2 1/2-hour practice can be used for those skills.

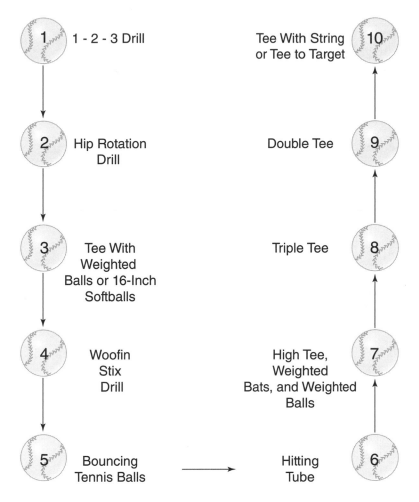

Figure 2   Sample 10-station circuit.

Timing the Circuit

For the hitting circuit, a manager or an injured player can serve as the time-keeper. The timekeeper has a stopwatch and a whistle. At the beginning of each station (6-minute period), the timekeeper blows the whistle and says "Begin." At the 2 1/2-minute mark, the timekeeper blows the whistle and says "Switch partners." At the 5-minute mark, the timekeeper blows the whistle twice and says, "Pick up the balls and equipment and change stations." In 1 hour with 10 groups in a 10-station circuit, each hitter should get 2 1/2 minutes of hitting at each station. This time allows each player 20 to 25 reps at each station, giving the player a total of 200 to 250 swings that day. Coaches should stress that they want quality not quantity. For the other 2 1/2 minutes at the station, the hitter is tossing, setting balls on the tee, or using other methods to assist her partner. The minute between stations gives the two partners time to pick up balls and move to the next station.

Figure 3 Sample 2 1/2-Hour Practice Plan

Step 1 (1:00–1:20pm)

Team stretches and warms up arms

Step 2 (1:20–1:40pm)

Team works on individual skills by position:

- Catcher and pitcher drills
- Infielder drills
- Outfielder drills

Step 3 (1:40–2:00pm)

Team works on special defensive drills:

- Defending the short game (10 minutes)
- Cutoff plays (10 minutes)

Step 4 (2:00–2:30pm)

Team works on live defensive situation drills

Step 5 (2:30–3:00pm)

Ten players complete hitting circuit training in batting cages. Ten players hit live on the field.

Step 6 (3:00–3:30pm)

Hitters in the cage go to live pitching on the field. Those on the field hit circuits in the cage.

Hands-On Teaching or Coaching Points

By positioning three coaches on the circuit, with each coach staying at a specific station, the staff can see every player get 20 to 25 reps. The coach's feedback is really important to the player and can lead to immediate results. The younger the player, the more the coach needs to get involved in the process. For instance, when using the Bouncing Tennis Balls drill or drills that involve front toss, the feeding tasks may be difficult for younger players. Coaches can perform the bounce and the toss while still coaching the hitter on every repetition. Outside of live hitting, circuit training is the best way to improve hitting skills.

Circuit Training for All Offensive Strategies

Circuit training can be used to work on all offensive skills and strategies. The circuit does not have to include 10 stations. For example, to work on bunting and to ensure that players get lots of reps, a coach could set up 5 stations: (1) sacrifice bunt off a machine, (2) sacrifice bunt off live pitching, (3) push bunt off a front toss, (4) push bunt off live pitching, and (5) bunt for a hit off live pitching. Stations can be designed for anything the team needs to work on. Circuit training allows coaches to incorporate a lot of reps into the time allotted.

Player Feedback

In circuit training, the players receive immediate feedback. If batters are trying to stay on the ball and hit it up the middle, they can see the path of the ball into the net. If they are trying to cut a loop out of their swing using a double tee (high, low), they will see immediate success or failure. In the Wall Swing drill, if the players hit the net, they know they are not keeping their hands inside the ball.

Appendix B:
Poor Man's Circuit

Despite the title, this circuit applies to male or female coaches. The males do not have a monopoly on budget restraints. We came up with this circuit when coaching at a small college with next to no budget. We wanted to have a basic circuit system, but we could not afford to spend a lot of money. The Poor Man's Circuit described here provides ideas that do not cost a lot of money to implement.

We often hear coaches say, "I cannot afford circuit training." All coaches can and should use circuit training. Many circuits can be created with little or no cost, and these circuits still provide the training that enables a player to become a strong hitter. Some of the greatest hitters in the games of softball and baseball had humble beginnings and could not afford to purchase expensive equipment or training devices. In the early days of the game, the ball was a sock surrounded by tape, and the bats were wooden. The wooden bats would break and splinter, but players would just put nails in them, wrap them in electrical tape, and use them forever. The best coaches and players are those who find a way to train and do not let the lack of fancy equipment or training devices hamper their progress. Of course, there are some great devices on the market, and they are very useful for training. However, for coaches who are just starting a team or those who need help until they can afford the desired training equipment, the ideas in the Poor Man's Circuit can be used to provide effective training.

STATION 1: TEE DRILL, STANDING

Purpose Hitting off a tee allows the batter to get a lot of repetitions in a confined space (using a net to catch the balls). Coaches can specify what part of the swing they want the players to work on and can vary it throughout the practice session.

Execution Set up a tee at the appropriate height for the batter to stand at. The batter takes up her normal batting stance and executes the swing—load, stride, contact, extension, and finish. Do 20 repetitions.

Coaching Points For teams with a limited supply of softballs, this drill can be done without balls. The batter addresses the tee and swings through, lightly touching the top of the tee. A coach can think up a lot of drills using a basic tee.

STATION 2: TEE DRILL, KNEELING

Purpose This drill isolates the upper body. It is amazing how much better the batter's hands become when the upper body is isolated. When Ralph was a coach for the 1996 Olympic team, one of the best players in the world did 25 reps of each of these kneeling drills every day before doing any other hitting.

Execution Use a regular tee that may not have a serviceable stem. The tee must be short enough so that the batter can make contact when she is kneeling. The right-handed batter kneels on her right knee, and the left-handed batter kneels on her left knee. The batter swings through the ball from this position, isolating the upper body (figure 1). For maximum effectiveness, batters can do 20 swings with her right arm, 20 swings with her left arm, and 20 regular swings with both arms.

Coaching Points The coach should watch for proper upper-body mechanics in the swing, making sure that the batter's swing path is correct, that the batter has the correct hand position (palm up, palm down) at contact, and that she finishes long after contact.

Figure 1 Batting from a kneeling position.

Variation When using her regular bat, the batter may need to choke up in order to maintain control of the barrel (figure 1). A variation of this drill is to use a shorter and lighter bat. We have a 26-inch, 18-ounce bat that some batters use for this drill. If a batter is not strong enough to properly swing a regular size bat with just one arm, she will tend to drop the barrel and cast or sweep. The focus of one-arm drills is proper mechanics, not hitting the ball hard, so a batter should use whatever size bat is necessary to ensure that her mechanics remain sound throughout the drill. The batter should take 10 reps with each hand. Always make sure that the tee is set at the proper contact point for drill work. Unless the batter is working on inside or outside pitches, the tee should be placed even with the front foot, and from there the batter should be hitting every ball up the middle.

STATION 3: BOUNCING TENNIS BALLS

This drill (see chapter 4, page 78) is a must have station for any hitting circuit because it enables batters to work on load, stride, and swing. Get some old tennis balls from a tennis coach and you are in business.

STATION 4: HIGH TEE

High Tee on Home Plate is described in chapter 5 (see page 99). This is the same drill, but it is now done in a batting cage with a catch net. The High Tee on Home Plate drill is key to teaching batters the correct hand path and helping them learn not to allow their hands to drop or loop. If you don't have a tee that will extend high enough, set a tee on a milk carton or an old bucket. Set the tee even with the batter's chest. The batter should take a regular swing, keeping her hands inside the ball. This is a drill that players can also do one handed. The older the players, the better they will be able to perform the drill using one hand.

Coaching Points   High Tee drills are great for teaching batters where to strike the ball in order to get loft and distance. These drills also help batters feel the palm-up, palm-down position at contact. Teach batters to watch the spin on the ball as it travels into the net. The batter wants to create backspin because this will keep the ball in the air longer. Front- or downspin will result in ground balls and is an indication that the batter is rolling her wrists at contact.

STATION 5: HITTING TUBE

The Hitting Tube drill is described in chapter 6 (see page 108). For teams that can't afford to buy an expensive tube, several substitutes can be used to perform this drill. Coaches can hang a tire from a tree. Or they can get an old handheld tackling dummy from a football coach, put some weights in it, and wrap it with duct tape. The drill simply requires a hanging device that provides resistance as the batter makes contact. This drill helps batters build wrist strength.

STATION 6: Z-LINE DRIVE

Purpose   This drill teaches the batter to get the barrel on plane with the pitch early and to keep the barrel on plane for as long as possible.

Execution   Take a 50-foot (15.2 m) electrical cord, cut off the male and female ends, and load it with five Wiffle balls by putting the cord through the center holes of each Wiffle ball. Put a hook on each end of the cord so that the cord can be attached between two sturdy devices, such as a fence or pole. Some people use the volleyball stanchions with eyelets because these are easy to hook the cord onto. Coating the cord with WD-40 will help to achieve speed on the ball. With all of the balls on one end of the cord, the batter moves one ball to her contact point (see figure 2). She takes a normal swing, hitting the top half (the half above the electrical cord) of the ball and sending it down to the other end. Once all of the balls are hit, the batter walks to the other end and hits them back. Do 20 repetitions.

Figure 2   Batting on the Z-line.

Coaching Points   This drill reveals immediately if the batter doesn't get her barrel on plane with the ball early or if she struggles to keep the barrel on plane. If she brings the barrel to the ball in a downward arc, she will strike the cord, and it will "bounce" a lot as the ball is hit. The ball won't travel as fast down the cord. If the barrel is on plane, the cord will bounce very little. Players like the Z-Line Drive drill because they never have to pick up softballs!

Variation   To really challenge the batter, a teammate or coach can stand at one end with all of the balls and "pitch" them to the batter at the other end by pushing the ball down the line. The pitcher must make sure she doesn't push down on the cord when sending the ball to the batter. Pushing down on the cord will create unrealistic movement on the ball and make it impossible to hit.

STATION 7: WALL SWING

This drill is described in chapter 2 (see page 41) for slappers, and a slight variation for other hitters is discussed in appendix A (see page 164). In this circuit, a gym wall protector or a fence is used instead of a net. The batter should place the nub of the bat against her belly button and place the head of the bat against the fence or wall. From a normal batting stance, the batter swings through without a ball involved. If the batter casts or sweeps, she will hit the fence or the wall padding. Instant feedback!

STATION 8: SMALL WIFFLE BALLS AND BROOMSTICK

Purpose This is a very good drill for helping batters improve their focus.

Execution Commercial stick bats are available but a similar tool can be created by cutting a broomstick or dowel to the length of the batter's bat. Tape the handle with athletic tape. Buy a couple dozen golf-ball-size Wiffle balls. From a kneeling position, the coach tosses the Wiffle balls to the batter, who drives them into a catch net or blanket (see figure 3). Do 20 repetitions.

Coaching Points Make sure the batters maintain their fundamentals while trying to hit the much smaller balls.

Variation A variation involves using two different colored Wiffle balls. The coach calls out the color of the one that the batter should hit.

Figure 3 Stick bat and small Wiffle ball.

STATION 9: 1-2-3 DRILL

The 1-2-3 Drill is described in chapter 5 (see page 96). The batter focuses on sound swing mechanics without actually hitting a ball. This drill only requires a mirror and a bat. If outdoors, the coach can provide the feedback that the mirror would provide. The batter takes up her stance. She loads on the command of "one," strides on the command of "two," and swings on the command of "three." The coach or batter looks for proper stance, load, stride, and finish to the swing. During the drill, the coach can stop the batter at any phase and check her body positioning.

STATION 10: PITCH RECOGNITION

The Pitch Recognition drill is described in chapter 4 (see page 75). To vary the drill, the batter can call out "yes" or "no" to communicate whether or not she would have swung at the pitch. We generally have three or four batters rotating through, each taking a simulated at-bat before switching with another batter. They will stay at this station for 15 to 20 minutes. Make sure the batter's body is positioned just as it would be in a real game. Players can get lazy when they know they are not actually going to hit the ball. To take full advantage of this drill, the batter should perform every phase of the swing realistically, except she shouldn't bring the barrel to the ball.

Appendix C: 150 Swings for Success

This is a simple program we began teaching at camps and clinics over 15 years ago. It takes about 25 minutes to complete and requires the batter to work on every part of the hitting cycle during the workout. We advise players to do these 150 swings five times a week. The only equipment needed for these drills is a tee, a bat, and 25 Wiffle balls. Use baseball-size Wiffle balls to increase the focus required to perform the skills. Players can even do these drills in their basement, carport, or backyard. When performing the drills indoors, players should use a mirror if possible so they can watch their fundamentals. Here are the six stations. Batters complete 25 repetitions at each station to complete the total 150 swings for success:

- **Station 1: 1-2-3 Drill.** (See chapter 5, page 96.) The batter sets up in her stance and takes 25 swings, attempting to make each swing as perfect as she can. Watching these swings in a mirror is very beneficial to the player.

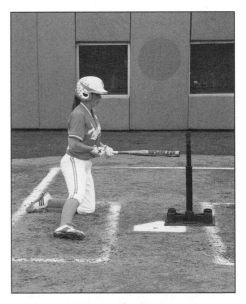

- **Station 2: Kneeling Wall Drill.** This drill is a variation of the Wall Swing drill in chapter 2 (see page 41). In this version, the batter is positioned on one knee and uses the tee as the barrier (some coaches refer to this drill as the anti-sweep drill; see figure 1). The batter kneels, places the nub of the bat against her belly button, and places the head of the bat touching or nearly touching the tee. The batter takes 25 swings, keeping the bat inside the tee. If the batter sweeps or casts, she knocks down the tee.

Figure 1 Position for batter.

- **Station 3: One-Arm, Kneeling Backhand Drill.** The batter kneels and takes 25 one-arm backhand swings (i.e., she swings with the lead hand). The batter works on keeping her hand inside the ball and following through.

- **Station 4: One-Arm, Kneeling Forehand Drill.** The batter kneels and takes 25 one-arm forehand swings (i.e., she swings with the power hand). Again, the batter is working on keeping her hand inside the ball and following through (figure 2).

- **Station 5: Kneeling Two-Hand Drill.** The batter takes 25 swings, working on the entire upper-body sequence from the kneeling position: loading, leading with the backhand arm, staying inside the ball, staying long through the ball, and finishing high or extended.

Figure 2 Batting with the forehand.

- **Station 6: Standing Tee With Normal Swing.** The batter finishes with 25 swings from a standing position at the tee. She uses a full-body swing, executing every sequence of the swing cycle.

Many players find that their batting average and ability to hit for power improve tremendously after only six months of working consistently with these drills.

About the Authors

Ralph and **Karen Weekly** are head coaches at the University of Tennessee, where they have led the Lady Vols to 514 wins since 2002. The duo has celebrated over 1,700 combined career victories and received numerous honors, including being named SEC Coach of the Year twice and the NFCA Region Coaching Staff of the Year in 2005, 2007, and 2010. They have led Tennessee to four top three national finishes in the annual Women's College World Series, to four NCAA Regional and Super Regional Championships, and have participated in the SEC Tournament nine times, including four championships. The two led Pacific Lutheran University to NAIA national championship titles in 1988 and 1992 and were named National Coaches of the Year during that time. The duo has had 40 All-SEC or All-Freshman selections, 34 Louisville Slugger/NFCA All Region selections, 21 Louisville Slugger/NFCA All-America selections, and 12 CoSIDA/Capital One Academic All-American selections.

Ralph Weekly enters his 11th season at Tennessee with a prestigious new accolade to include on his already impressive resume: The National Fastpitch Coaches Association (NFCA) recently honored his efforts in a distinguished three-decade career with a 2011 induction into the NFCA Hall of Fame. During his 24-year coaching career, Ralph has been successful at every stop, amassing 1,015 overall collegiate victories and championships in both armed forces as well as international softball. Ralph has coached teams including the U.S. Air Force, Pacific Lutheran University, University of Tennessee at Chattanooga, and University of Tennessee. He was the hitting coach for the 1996 and 2000 U.S. Olympic softball teams, both of which received gold medals. From 1993 to 2000, he coached (as head or assistant coach) in 13 international events, winning the gold medal in each of them.

Karen Weekly has experienced success both on the field and off, earning awards as a player and a coach. While at Pacific Lutheran University, she was an All-American softball player, led NAIA hitters with a .440 batting average, and was named Female Athlete of the Year. She was a national title-winning assistant coach at PLU in 1988 and 1992 and served as a championship head coach at the University of Tennessee at Chattanooga. A 15-year collegiate softball head coaching veteran boasting 737 career wins, Karen Weekly is in her 11th season with her husband, Ralph, at the helm of the Lady Volunteer softball program.